The Future of **Family Farms**

D1287086

WITHDRAWN

THE FUTURE OF
Family Farms

Practical Farmers' Legacy Letter Project

TERESA OPHEIM

UNIVERSITY OF IOWA PRESS

Iowa City

Urbandale Public Library
3520-86th Street
Urbandale, IA 50322

University of Iowa Press, Iowa City 52242
Copyright © 2016 by the University of Iowa Press
www.uiowapress.org
Printed in the United States of America

Design by Richard Hendel

No part of this book may be reproduced or used in any form or by any means
without permission in writing from the publisher. All reasonable steps have been
taken to contact copyright holders of material used in this book. The publisher
would be pleased to make suitable arrangements with any whom it has not been
possible to reach.

The University of Iowa Press is a member of Green Press Initiative
and is committed to preserving natural resources.

Printed on acid-free paper

Library of Congress Cataloging-in-Publication Data
Names: Opheim, Teresa, 1961– author.
Title: The future of family farms : Practical Farmers' legacy letter
project / Teresa Opheim.
Other titles: Practical Farmers' legacy letter project
Description: Iowa City : University of Iowa Press, [2016] | Includes
bibliographical references and index.
Identifiers: LCCN 2016007491 | ISBN 978-1-60938-453-1 (pbk) |
ISBN 978-1-60938-454-8 (ebk)
Subjects: LCSH: Family farms. | Farm ownership.
Classification: LCC HD1476.A3 O64 2016 | DDC 338.1—dc23
LC record available at http://lccn.loc.gov/2016007491

All photographs courtesy of Practical Farmers of Iowa, except for page 22 courtesy
of Kathryn Ruhf, page 66 photo by Helen D. Gunderson, page 82 courtesy of Neil
Hamilton, and page 94 courtesy of Constance Falk.

To the members of Practical Farmers of Iowa

We come and go, but the land is always here.

And the people who love it and understand it,

are the people who own it—for a little while.

—WILLA CATHER, *O Pioneers!*

CONTENTS

ACKNOWLEDGMENTS

Every year, the members of Practical Farmers of Iowa (PFI) volunteer their time, share what they have learned, and offer their hard-earned dollars. As you will see from reading these farm transfer stories from members, these are wonderful people. Thank you, first of all, to all PFI members.

It is hard for many people to go public with their stories, and yet they do, because they want to help others. Thank you to these members who have shared what matters most and how they are achieving their farm transfer goals: Jon Bakehouse, Marietta Carr, Mary Damm, Del Ficke, Irene Frantzen, James Frantzen, Tom Frantzen, Jim French, Lisa French, John Gilbert, Helen Gunderson, Twyla Hall, Neil Hamilton, Chris Henning, Leon Isakson, Marilyn Isakson, Erwin Johnson, Wendy Johnson, Yoshiko Johnson, Jane Juchems, Rick Juchems, Susan Jutz, Fred Kirchenmann, Jeff Klinge, Linda Lynch, Robert Lynch, Cindy Madsen, Vic Madsen, Margaret McQuown, Chris Mohr, Darrel Mohr, Dale Nimrod, Barb Opheim, Wayne Opheim, James Petersen, Mark Peterson, Melanie Peterson, Dick Schwab, Charlotte Shivvers, Martha Skillman, Phil Specht, Mary Swander, Angela Tedesco, Deb Tidwell, Steve Turman, Dan Wilson, and Angela Winburn.

Thank you to the PFI Board of Directors for allowing me to work on this book. All proceeds will come back to PFI. In 2015 those directors were Ann Cromwell, Kathy Eckhouse, Ann Franzenburg, Tyler Franzenburg, Gail Hickenbottom, Wendy Johnson, Vic Madsen, Mark Peterson, Mark Quee, David Rosmann, Kurt Van Hulzen, and Dan Wilson.

And thank you to the PFI Farm Transfer Committee, which helps set directions for the farm transfer programming: Irene Frantzen,

Tom Frantzen, Kate Edwards, Heather Holcomb, Cindy Madsen, Vic Madsen, Margaret Smith, Dan Wilson, and Angela Winburn.

I worked with a terrific staff over my ten years as the executive director of PFI. Thank you to all of them! A particular thanks to the three I worked with the longest: Sarah Carlson, Suzi Howk, and Sally Worley.

Finally, with gratitude to my partner, Rich Schuler, who taught me to look to the skies; my son, Paul Opheim (how did I get so lucky to have a child like this?); and my farmland-owning parents, Barb and Wayne Opheim, who gave me the gift of a stable and loving home.

Farmland Transfer
What Matters Most?

All the Things I Could Tell You *by Teresa Opheim*

How much I have learned from the members of Practical Farmers of Iowa! In so many ways, so many times. While I served as the executive director of this organization—a member-driven nonprofit that strengthens farms and communities through farmer-led investigation and information sharing—from 2006 to 2016, I learned how complex farming with nature can be. I learned what it takes to produce food with the attributes I want. I learned patience and commitment to family, to farmland, to continuity, to community, and more.

I am still learning, and in no area more than farmland transfer.

About five years ago, a farmer stopped me at a field day, one of our frequent on-farm open houses where farmers share information about their farming practices, and confided he worried whether his son would be able to continue farming. The farmer's landowning mother had just died, and her farmland was being divided among her children. At other field days since, farmers without farming children reported being sad they hadn't found the right young people to continue their operations. Many confided about rancor among siblings once their parents passed, even though the family had always gotten along well before. One particularly reticent farmer muttered to me: "All the things I could tell you.... All the things I could tell you ..." And he drifted off, shaking his head.

Mary Swander brilliantly illustrated much of the drama surrounding farm transfer in her play, *Map of My Kingdom*. As she explains in the essay included here, she traveled the countryside gathering stories; soon the word was out, and the stories started coming to her. There were "some common archetypal, even biblical, scenarios," she reports. "The Cain and Abel story repeated itself—one family member coming to blows with another over their piece of land. The return of the prodigal son story also came up again and again—a relative returning to the farm after a long estrangement or absence, only to try to claim his inheritance."

Whatever the themes, we are in for a lot of drama in the coming years. According to Iowa State University, 35 percent of Iowa farmland is owned by those over seventy-five years of age; 56 percent is owned by people over the age of sixty-five.[1] About 10 percent of all farmland is expected to change hands within the next five years alone, according to the U.S. Department of Agriculture.[2]

This book is not about farm *business* transfers; Kathryn Ruhf, the senior program director for Land for Good, based in Keene, New Hampshire, explains in her essay the myriad complexities of that and why land access, tenure, and transfer are serious issues for the future of American agriculture. The book is simply about *farmland*—how families acquired it, what they treasure most about it, and their hopes for its future. At Practical Farmers of Iowa, we have discovered through discussions at field days, workshops, and play performances that too often farmland owners move to put in place a strategy (such as form a trust or buy life insurance) before deciding what they want most for their farmland in the future. The stories in this book, which grew out of our Farm Legacy Letter project, are an attempt to help farmland owners slow down and think through goals. The book is not about the strategies they will use to achieve those farmland goals.

The Future of Family Farms includes farmland owners whose families have owned a particular patch of the earth since the 1800s, as well as a woman who purchased farmland in 2015. Farmers tell some of these stories; other stories are from those who grew up on the farm and never came back. The book even features *former* farmland owners, because—after careful thought about what mattered most to them—these individuals sold their land. Most of the stories come straight from farmland owners themselves; others are told through profiles and interviews.

DECIDING WHAT'S MOST IMPORTANT

I deeply admire Tom and Irene Frantzen of northern Iowa, and am thankful for their leadership and example in addressing farm transfer issues. They have done something so many others have not: spent the time to think through what they want for their farm's future, and then communicated those goals to their heirs as well as publicly to help others. The Frantzens' farm transfer goal is the "long-term protection for a true Iowa family farm that has significant conservation features blended into a working landscape."

As Tom and Irene hit their late fifties, they began thinking seriously about their farm legacy. The Frantzens are followers of Holistic Management, which they used as the driver as they worked out the details of their generational transfer. As Tom says, "The basic principle in Holistic Management is that we have no idea where we're going if we don't have goals."

Tom says that once you set those goals, then actions can follow. At their basic essence, most farmland owners' top goals for their farmland include:

- Keep family harmony
- Provide land for my farming heir(s) to farm
- Provide a farm for a family to work
- Help provide my heirs with greater financial stability through the sale of, or rental income from, the farm
- Use my farmland to benefit a charitable cause
- Give all of my heirs an inheritance of equal economic value
- Keep the farmland in my family
- Use the farmland for conservation

Dale Nimrod's story is one of my favorites in this collection. His parents purchased a farm in southwest Iowa in 1944, but his father died before he had an opportunity to work the place. His mother was determined to raise her family on the farm, a feat Dale thinks would have been very difficult without the support of the small town of Stanton and the local church. None of the three Nimrod children grew up to be farmers; years later, they decided the best way to pay back that community was to "find a nice young family who would appreciate the land, the community, and the church, and would invest themselves in caring for all three."

Finding the right family involved sleuthing and then putting together a generous and innovative financing plan. "It is a misperception, I think, that selling to the highest bidder is the only way to be fair when disposing of property," Dale says.

Neil Hamilton also grew up on and then inherited a farm in southwest Iowa and also chose to sell to a beginning farmer. Says Neil:

Adams County needs young farmers owning a piece of land more than it needs people who used to live there hanging on to farmland pretending they're still farmers. As John Baker of the Beginning Farmer Center says: "You don't own a farm; you own a piece of farmland. It stopped being a farm when your family left it." A farm is a family, a piece of land, a business, an entity. People need to recognize that.

For Dale Nimrod and Neil Hamilton, a strong motivation was to keep farmers on the land and rural communities vibrant. For other farmland owners, environmental stewardship trumps other goals. Margaret McQuown's college graduation present was a one-way ticket to New York City to work as a fashion stylist for the Vogue/Butterick Pattern Company. She loved her career and the city life, but in 2012, after inheriting family farmland, she moved back home with her husband, Steve Turman. The farm her great-grandfather had named Pleasant Prospects Farms became Resilient Farms. Maggie and Steve have planted trees and shrubs to help restore a riparian buffer. They have restored a pond, fought invasive species, and plan to add grassed waterways rather than build or rebuild terraces.

Mary Damm is the most recent farmland owner in the book. Her friend Dan Specht, a longtime beloved member of Practical Farmers of Iowa, died in a farm accident in 2013. She has purchased much of his farm on the bluffs of the Mississippi River to manage it the way Dan would have, with a focus on habitat for grassland birds. "Dan wanted to show that farms can feed people and be a place for nature, that working farms and conservation can go together. . . . I will try to maintain the integrity of the grasslands and improve biodiversity and habitat, just like Dan was trying to do. That is my hope."

NOT NOSTALGIA

Recently I gave a talk about Practical Farmers of Iowa and included photos of Tim Smith and Dick Sloan, who grow corn and soybeans with cover crops like rye to keep the soil covered. I also included a photo of the Dan and Lorna Wilson family, whose enterprises include corn, beans, oats, hay, beef and dairy cattle, sheep, hogs, chickens, and vegetables. After the talk, an octogenarian agronomy professor commented that I was just being "nostalgic for an old way of farming." It turns out he thought any farmer who had enterprises other than corn and soybeans was out of step, simply longing for a time now gone.

In many of the stories recounted here, we see the march from more crops to fewer, a journey away from hard work and self-reliance and toward convenience. The experience of my mother, Barb Opheim, is common: When she was growing up in the 1930s and 1940s, her parents raised oats, soybeans, corn, hay, chickens, hogs, sheep, and dairy and beef cattle. They also tended a large vegetable garden, apple trees, and extensive flower beds.

Today, my mother's tenant raises two crops: corn and soybeans.

With that loss of plant and animal diversity came an increase in the use of chemicals. Fred Kirschenmann's father was deeply committed to conservation on his North Dakota farm. "My father somehow understood, intuitively, that the Dust Bowl was not just about the weather (which most of his neighbors assumed) but that it was also about the way farmers farmed. So he began to plant trees, and to keep fields relatively small and arranged in crop rotations so they were not as exposed to the wind. 'It was Roosevelt who taught us how to farm because of his soil erosion programs,' he said, even though he was a Republican!"

But in the 1950s, Fred's father began applying fertilizer. Says Fred: "Wheat was the best cash crop and adding fertilizer increased yields without crop rotations, so he started to raise more wheat. Then he had more weeds because of the reduced crop rotation. Then he started using herbicides to take care of the weeds."

There is, however, a theme of *increased* diversity and *decreased* chemical use in these stories as well. (Not surprisingly, as these stories come from members of Practical Farmers of Iowa, an organization that works toward an ecological rather than industrial model of agriculture.) When Fred took over the farm in 1976, he transformed it into one of the nation's most well-known organic and biodynamic farms. Nebraskan Del Ficke writes that he is improving native pastures and restoring and improving the soils "back to the way God intended."

Vic and Cindy Madsen made the same journey back toward more crops and no chemicals. Says Cindy: "We have an organic operation because we like to build soil health. We also think it is important to have livestock on the farm. If you have livestock, you have the manure to provide a natural fertilizer for the soil. The small grains and clover prepare the field for the corn. The beans following corn put nitrogen in the soil to feed the small grains. We feed the corn to the livestock. The livestock manure then feeds the crop ground again. It's a more sustainable circle."

One with practical benefits as well: "When you have grains and livestock, you are busy year-round. Plus, with so many enterprises, we balance the debt flow during the year. If you have a failure in one area, hopefully the other enterprises will make up for that failure," Cindy says.

Vic describes an added benefit: "When [sons] Jeff and Mark were about eight and ten, we had seeded some oats. We were out there digging in the ground to see how deep the seeds were. And that was fun. The boys wanted to do it with the corn too, but I couldn't let them because of the insecticide on the corn. I can still see how sad they were that they couldn't dig for the seed."

Perhaps no one in the collection has increased farmland diversity as much as Angela Tedesco, who, with her husband, John, purchased bare ground in central Iowa and raised hundreds of varieties of more than thirty types of vegetables and fruit for her vegetable subscription service, Community Supported Agriculture. In her story of providing food to 180 families, she describes the perks in sensory detail:

> *Dewdrops on leaf margins and spiderwebs. Birds of all kinds—*
> *from bluebirds and barn swallows to white pelicans and raptors—*
> *overhead.... The sounds of the meadowlarks and killdeer in the*
> *spring and the hawks screeching overhead, raindrops on the hoop-*
> *house plastic, and the clicking of the stirrup or wheel hoe as it*
> *moves through the soil.... The aroma of basil if brushed and other*
> *herbs from rosemary to lavender, a barn full of freshly harvested*
> *garlic and ripe strawberries in the heat of the day.*

Nostalgia? No, these are not stories of a wistful desire for a former time in one's life, a sentimental yearning for the happiness of a former place. Instead, they are about examining what is important, the lessons we have learned, and what we want to keep, to change, to let go. Many of the farmland owners in this book discovered they had thrown away too much that is valuable about agri*culture*, and they made amends. They hope to leave a legacy that continues those changes.

At the end of life, what stands out? That is what matters most, and

Rebecca Graff and husband, Tom Ruggieri, are among the farmers supplying the strong demand for local foods, including fresh fruits and vegetables. Horticultural production is a good way for the next generation to get into farming, as these operations generally require fewer acres of that very expensive farmland. Rebecca and Tom farm on Rebecca's father's land near Kearney, Missouri.

for these farmland owners, the land has provided much of that: a place for family, for skill and character building, for purpose. Cindy Madsen tells a poignant story about the effect of a single visit to their farm:

> *A while back, the group of us in Audubon County Family Farms hired a tour bus from the Des Moines Farmers Market. A grandfather and his two-year-old grandson were on the bus. At our place, the grandfather took a picture of this little boy in the bean field. The grandfather talked a lot about that trip to our farm. About a year later, the little boy's mother came to my booth at the farmers market and told me that the grandfather had passed away. In his casket, they included the picture of the little boy in the bean field because visiting our farm meant so much to the grandfather.*

We must acknowledge, however, that there has been huge loss in the countryside and in agriculture.

Helen Gunderson was the first to receive a Practical Farmers' Farmland Owner Award, now given yearly to farmland owners who do not labor on the land they own but who still work for vibrant rural communities and environmental stewardship of that land. (Other winners include the Shivvers sisters and the Nimrod family, whose stories are also included in this book.) Helen's ancestors purchased farmland in Pocahontas County, Iowa, in 1878. At one point, her father oversaw 3,200 acres for the family. She inherited 560 of those acres.

When Helen was young, there were eleven farmsteads along her five-mile road. "Each place had a family that lived on it and farmed the land," she writes in her documentary project *The Road I Grew Up On*.[3] "Each farm was nestled in a grove of trees with buildings such as corncribs, barns or silos. Each had animals such as Hereford cattle, Hampshire hogs, Shropshire sheep or Leghorn chickens. Each had a dog or cats that would hang around when the cows were milked. Many of the places had windmills that pumped water for farm and household use. Most of the families had large vegetable gardens."

Today, there are just three houses occupied on the road. Two of the farms have only a lone crib or a set of grain bins to mark the spot where a family once was part of the neighborhood. Five building sites have been completely cleared and cultivated. There is no prairie except remnants along the railroad tracks and in road ditches. Almost all the tillable land is in corn and soybeans, the so-called cash crops. There are no more horses, dogs, sheep, or chickens.

Through the years, Helen photographed and videotaped all the farmsteads, both occupied and abandoned. She interviewed the families along the road, in addition to the people who moved away. She documented the demolition of the house where her great-grandparents and grandparents lived. She documented the razing of buildings, the removal of fences, the removal of a mile of dirt road, the last hay field, the last cattle and pigs, the first tractor with caterpillar treads used for tillage, and the first genetically modified seeds as evidenced by new corporate seed signs posted along the road.

"When I recall the key tragic events that have brought the nation together to face death and grieve, my first thought is of the funeral procession for President John F. Kennedy with the harnessed, yet riderless, coal black horse," Helen writes. The Twin Towers falling in Manhattan, the bombing of the Oklahoma City federal building—these stark tragedies bring people together.

The loss in rural America is also spectacular, but it has evolved for more than a century, she says. "This gradual change involves the death of an era and the loss of a way of life, but here there are no collective rituals designed to provide comfort."

In the 1920s, my grandparents, Carl and Selma Opheim, were busy working a northwest Iowa farm Carl's father owned, and raising eight children when their world fell apart. In 1929, the stock market crashed, the Bode State Bank failed, and the family lost the farm.

"They lost so much," my dad, Wayne Opheim, reports, "and my family became so poor. I always wondered about the psychological effect of losing so much." Wayne was born later that year, and the family moved into town. "My dad then worked as a janitor at the Lutheran Church. I think the church felt sorry for him having all those kids and no job. In 1936, he applied for a job at the Bode schools. He came home one day and said, 'I got the job!' We all cheered. And he was a school janitor for the rest of his life."

Twenty miles away, my mother's farming family thrived, and it is on this farm (just miles from Helen's) that my grandparents spoiled me when I was young. As with so many families, no one in the next generation wanted to farm, and my grandparents eventually moved into town. Over the years, I watched the farm I knew disappear—the chicken coop, the flower beds, the gardens, the apple trees (one for each grandchild), and the extensive windbreak we dubbed "Fisher Woods." Toward the end of my grandmother's life, a neighboring farmer bought the homeplace, but he left it standing until she died. Then, one day, my mother and I cried as we drove by to see neighbors demolishing the house. About five years ago, all that was left were two trees in the ditches. Now there are none. A farm obliterated, as if our lives there had never happened.

I do not feel nostalgic about the farm; I just want to acknowledge its importance and that I am very sorry about its loss. I love working with and supporting farmers, but I do not want to farm myself or live on the family farmland that I will inherit with my siblings.

I am glad my mother agreed to have her story in this book, as it started a conversation about the past and the future of our family farmland. When she told it to me, I learned her grandfather plowed the ground out of prairie. I learned that she would like us to keep the land, but if that doesn't work, she is fine if we sell it when she is gone. Most important, I was reminded that, as always, her top goal is to keep family harmony.

VACANT LAND?

A few years back, there was a sign posted on a fence on the east side of Interstate 35, not far from the big box retail stores marching north from the Des Moines area. "VACANT land for sale," the sign announced, even though the land was filled with rows of corn and a farmstead complete with a home, barn, and silos.

Members of Practical Farmers of Iowa would never describe farmland as "empty" or "vacant," even if they were facing the dilemma of whether to sell the land to pay for medical bills or retirement. And their hackles are raised when farmland is viewed as solely a financial investment. Of course, many people do view farmland in urbanizing areas as vacant, as land "waiting for a better use"; certainly the developers near Angela Tedesco's now suburban farm view it that way.

Farmland investment is big business. As *Forbes Magazine* pointed out, "farmland has solidly beaten the stock market since the late 1990s.... The next time you pass through Waterloo or Story City, show the guys in overalls some respect, even if they're not carrying pitchforks."[4] According to a *Wall Street Journal* article, the chief executive of one company reported that "softer farmland values are creating buying opportunities. A little bit of pain in farm country makes our job easier."[5]

The financial assets farmland owners have are breathtaking. I work with the most humble, down-to-earth farmers—who happen to own farmland worth $10 million and more. Northeast Iowa farmer Jeff Klinge points out in his story the negatives of high-priced land, including how hard the run-up in farmland values has been for beginning farmers:

> If we didn't have farm programs just for the farmers that specialize in those two crops [corn and soybeans], the price of land could fall by as much as 50 percent. The big landowners would be crying something terrible, but it would be a shot in the arm for beginning farmers if they only had to pay half as much for land.... High land prices are only good for somebody who's using farmland as an

*Farming is the chosen career path for many talented and smart young people
who are not from farm families, such as Kate Edwards of Iowa City, Iowa. Major
barriers for beginning farmers such as Edwards include the short-term leases that
many farmland owners offer and the high price of farmland.*

*investment to make money and not for the people who are actually
trying to make a living farming it.*

Less than half of the farmland owners in this book have a farming heir; those who do face a most vexing dilemma. As Iowa State
University professor emeritus of economics Mike Duffy explains, in
the United States today, most farmland owners have decided to give
their assets to their nonfarming and farming heirs in financially equal
shares. Unless a family has extensive off-farm resources, it will be
hard for the farming heir to pay off nonfarming heirs (or answer to
those who have contributed little to the farm over the years).

As Mike says, "If you have a child who spends his or her career
working the farm and helping take care of Mom, shouldn't there
be additional value in that? The responsibility of taking care of the
mother should be recognized. The responsibility of having built the
farming operation should be recognized. Equal and fair may not be

the same thing. If I want my child to continue to farm, I will give him more because I want to see the farm continued. That's why you need to decide what your goals are and prioritize your goals."

At Practical Farmers of Iowa, I see the "land tenure ladder," first written down in the 1920s, at work all the time. The ladder includes rungs like being an unpaid laborer on your parents' home farm, spending time as a tenant operator, becoming a mortgaged owner and then a full owner. As Neil Hamilton explains in his story:

> *Historically this nation's preference was not for tenancy but to convert tenants into owners. In the 1940s, tenancy was almost seen as an evil. There was the ladder you moved up from being a hired employee, to tenant, to being an owner. Ownership was the goal for a lot of reasons. For security. For wealth creation. For stewardship. Not many people would choose to always be a tenant if they could own the land.*

The story of the Shivvers sisters and the Petersens, included in this book, is a terrific example. Since the farm crisis of the 1980s, Jim Petersen established himself as a trustworthy farming partner by repaying a farm loan his family had received from the Shivverses' mother. Then in 2004, Jim began renting 160 acres of Shivvers land to transition it to organic. Again the relationship progressed, and in 2009 the Shivvers sisters sold (at a generous price) the land to the Petersens, who now have two children farming with them. Later they sold another 40 acres (and the Petersen family now rents and farms the remaining Shivvers-owned land). It was a long, patient process of farmland owners deciding what mattered most (conservation, allowing new farmers on the land) and then helping another family up that land tenure ladder.

Whether they have farming heirs or not, most of these farmland owners face tough decisions about their land's future. Kansas farmers Lisa and Jim French, for example, have two children who have chosen legal careers, and the Frenches know they need to do some soul-searching. Says Lisa:

> *Here is a conversation we need to have with our children: Should we sell part of our land? Will we have to? There may be some need to do so for their stability and for ours. We have just gone through the process of creating a trust. Every dime and piece of property*

Mary and Bill Beaman farm on land they own near Bedford, Iowa. They have one son who farms with them and four nonfarming daughters. Farmland owners with farming and nonfarming heirs may need to choose between two goals: Give all offspring an inheritance of equal financial value? Or provide land for the farming heir(s) to farm?

*we have could be needed to take care of us until we die. You wonder
how all that is going to work out. That hangs over you a bit.*

GRATITUDE

Several farmland owners, like Fred Kirschenmann and Margaret Mc-
Quown, predict extremely challenging times for our future. As Margaret's husband, Steve Turman, writes: "We are seeing that our biosphere has limits and that we are beginning to experience those; we
are realizing that we cannot have our planet and eat it too, so to speak.
One way or another, our future will include occupying this landscape
differently than we have for the past few centuries."

Despite all the concerns about the future and the complications
of deciding and implementing farmland goals and strategies, in the
end the essence of many of these stories is gratitude. "My parents
and grandparents provided me with such an amazing life," southwest
Iowa farmer Jon Bakehouse writes in his story. "There is such turmoil
in the world; I wish others could have what I have. Our son needs to
understand that he's very lucky, and he should be compassionate with
others."

Marilyn Isakson, from northern Iowa, wants her farmland to be remembered for "happy grandchildren learning about the garden and
having fun in the wide-open spaces. We treasure those days." Says Jim
French: "When we sit out on the deck at night, sipping our glass of
wine, we see our heritage and all who went before us. There is something so valuable in that continuity, embedded in the past and our
vision we want to see in the future."

This, from Irene Frantzen, is one of my favorites in the collection:

*I was by myself picking rocks in the field across the creek west of
the farmstead. I was near the edge of the field at the top of the hill
where we have a windbreak of border trees to the farm. I stopped
for a few minutes and sat on the grass by the trees and looked all
around. I had a great view of the fields, the house, the barn, the hoop
buildings, cattle in the pasture, the pond where ducks were wading
and geese were in sight. The birds were chirping. I took in the fresh
air, the green grass, and the daisy I had just picked.... I was meant
to be on a farm, raising a family, teaching them to appreciate
the beauty all around us.... I thought about what my father-in-
law would say if he were still here today. I know he would be very*

pleased to see that we carried on to another generation of loving the land and doing a good job of farming.

Tom Frantzen says: "This farm has a story that started 100 years ago.... Today our farm is profitable, and we provide sustainable employment. It is a good place to work and an important part of a rural community.... One hundred years ago, it was carved out of a chunk of tallgrass prairie, and it has been changed enormously in many different ways since."

Irene, sitting on her hillside, wonders about the farm after she and Tom are gone: "Will the farm look the same? Will it have even more diversity? Will our family descendants be farming it?"

Of course, none of us knows, let alone the farmland owners included in this book. But they hope that by sharing their farmland legacies, they will encourage others to ponder and then write the histories, accomplishments, challenges, and hopes for their farmland, for the generations who come after they are gone.

How Important Is It for Beginning Farmers to Own Farmland? *by Members of Practical Farmers of Iowa*

A while back I asked the membership of Practical Farmers of Iowa for their thoughts on whether it is important for beginning farmers to own farmland. As always with the members of this organization, there were diverse and thoughtful comments.

SECURE LAND TENURE

Landownership must eventually be part of the package of farming, so a farmer can put up buildings and infrastructure to support production and build equity in an appreciating long-term asset.

However, it is better to have secure land tenure of buildings and adjacent farmland (even as a rental-only situation) rather than ownership of a small acreage without possibilities of expansion down the road. We are very grateful to the family members who agreed to rent us land and a farmstead to start our farm business. We don't have to tie up money in a mortgage on land or a house right away, so we can afford to take on the business debt of an operating loan for machinery and equipment. Our goal is to get our business established, gain skills, prove ourselves and our markets first. Someday, if we are able to buy land either down the road or across the county, we will have a track record of paying the annual rent bill on time, which could help show a banker we have an ability to repay a mortgage.

LANDOWNERSHIP BUILDS WEALTH

My husband and I would have a very hard time justifying buying our farm at its current appraised value. We'd also have a very hard time justifying how hard we've worked over the last eight years of farming if we didn't have at least some of the wealth from the appreciation of the value of our farm. Generally speaking, farmers should probably try and buy at least some of their land, except when land prices are in an unsustainable bubble, because the farmers are going to need to have their land appreciate in order to experience wealth creation.

DON'T LOCK UP DOLLARS IN LANDOWNERSHIP

In the world of row crops, I think there are strong economic reasons not to own. Many nonfarm businesses don't own their storefronts. Owning a commercial asset ties up capital that could otherwise be directed toward growing a business, buying more inventory, or opening a second store. This can apply to farming as well. Let's play with some imaginary numbers:

Imagine if a beginning farmer rented 300 acres of ground at $250/acre ($75,000/year). Compare that to buying the same 300 acres for $6,500/acre ($1,950,000). Is the farmer better off owning or renting?

Since cash is king in any business, without locking up dollars into landownership, I think a farmer could rent more ground with the $1,950,000 not spent on ownership and increase his business, achieve more efficient use of equipment, and produce a higher income.

If, after a number of years of rigorous saving, that beginning farmer could afford to purchase farmland, it would seem to make more sense to purchase other ground, if he has a good partnership with a landlord on his rental ground.

MANY FARMS AND FARMERS

Our neighbor just died. His will dictated that the entire homestead (many nice barns and a good older house that had been well maintained for at least four generations of the same family) be destroyed. This way the land was ready for development in our sprawling metro area. His kids didn't have to make any hard decisions, as it was Dad's wishes that everything be destroyed. So they hired the neighbor to bulldoze it all. Even the trees are gone.

My other neighbors used the 1031 "like-kind" exchange program (Internal Revenue Code) and traded land in Polk County [the county Des Moines is in] to developers for land in Webster and Hamilton Counties. They avoided capital gains taxes and got 5,000 acres for 500. A lot of young people in Webster and Hamilton Counties who always thought that land would come available had to make new plans....

It is important for many small farmers to own small farms. It is what our democracy is based on, and it is the underlying foundation of our republic. It develops the type of character that has made Iowa a stand-out state. It also makes it more difficult to pack up and leave when the going gets tough.

LOW DEBT, SLOW GROWTH

As a beginning vegetable grower with no family land and little money, I don't think it's necessary for me to own land to be able to farm. There are many landowners who are willing to let me use their land, for free or for some sort of exchange, because they want to see it used and they want me to succeed. Many of these offers are impractical for one reason or another, but they indicate to me a general willingness to help beginning farmers without a real desire to benefit monetarily.

I've been reading Virginia farmer Joel Salatin's *You Can Farm*, and in it he talks about how landownership and the desire to find the perfect place to settle down can be a financial and emotional trap for a lot of people who want to farm. He suggests that we be more mobile in our thinking, that we not be so tied down by expensive, permanent infrastructure and retain the ability to move to a new farm. His prime example is grazing on rented land and how that can be far more profitable than buying land and grazing it.

Because I am not focused on buying land, I can farm in a low-debt, slow-growth way that fits my personality and abilities. I have more flexibility and less pressure. I may eventually want to buy land, but I could conceivably farm my whole adult life without buying land and still be able to have a profitable farm business.

LAND TRUST PROTECTS OWNERS

When I was on the board of a land trust, we owned the land, but any improvements were owned by the homeowner. The lease was ninety-nine years and could be passed on to family. If the homeowner decided to leave, the lease had to go to a family in a similar situation as defined by income levels, etc.... Using a land trust for a farm situation, I could have exclusive rights to the land, care for it, learn from it, and improve it. I would benefit from my improvements (such as soil building and animal fencing) for my natural life. I could even pass it along to a child. If I left, I could get my improvement costs back from the new farmer. I would even know that when I died, the land would stay in trust, be restricted, and benefit someone of the same criteria that I met when I started. The benefits I receive as a private farmland owner, I can also have as a land trust lessee. A land trust would not interfere with the "ownership" by the farmer if the leases were done properly.

THE TRADITIONAL FARMER 401K

Farmers should eventually be able to own at least some of their land, because it enables them to:

1. Get financing from a lender for infrastructure projects (to put up a grain bin, packhouse, machine shed, etc.). The value of financing is that it enables cash-strapped farmers to spread out a big fixed asset improvement cost over many years.
2. Have some security that if they put their money into an infrastructure project, they are making a safe investment (meaning, they know they can be on the property for years to come, and if/when they decide to sell the property, they may earn back some of the initial investment).
3. Turn an annual fee (rent) into an investment in an asset (farmland) that generally appreciates over the long term (the traditional farmer 401K). If you compare the cost of our market rate rent to what it would cost us to pay a mortgage on market rate farmland each year, this still holds true in most scenarios.

More farming families ought to be reaping the benefits of land values appreciating, not fewer!

Farm Dynasties *by Helen D. Gunderson*

I don't believe in farm dynasties. Perhaps there are instances where people of wealth who own land can enable farmers who use sustainable practices and don't have as much wealth to stay on the land. And certainly, in a country that honors freedom and capitalism, anyone who has enough money and desire can buy land, when it is available. However, what bothers me is the way landownership by the same family for many decades has been put on a pedestal even when the heirs have had little or no contact with the land and those who farm it. Iowa's Century Farm and Heritage Farm programs, which recognize families who have owned the same farmland for 100 and 150 years or more, do that. Our culture does, too. I never hear challenges to people living in some distant state talking about feeling connected to their heritage because they own farmland in the Midwest. Even though the economy and culture of my hometown of Rolfe were shaped by farming, I don't ever recall discussions in the schools, churches, organizations, or community about the issues of landownership.

With my rural farmland, I don't want to continue the family land dynasty that started with my great-grandfather and his brother. For the most part, my nieces and nephews have no connection to the land; presumably they are all doing well by their respective standards, and are likely to inherit land and/or other assets from their parents and others. Owning land should have something to do with being connected to that land—like knowing about the terrain, the people who farm it, and the ethics involved in managing it.

These days, there is talk of the great "income inequality" in our country. Trends in landownership and how land is used would seem to fall under that umbrella of issues. We should de-emphasize government programs like the Century and Heritage Farm awards, or at least establish additional programs that would honor landowners who rent or transfer their property to farmers or other people who would manage the land in healthy ways. Practical Farmers of Iowa has taken one step in that direction by initiating its annual Farmland Owner Award.

Two of my professors at San Francisco Theological Seminary taught about issues of landownership in their course on the Old Testament and the prophets. They used a big term called "latifundializa-tion," which means "process whereby land increasingly accrues into the hands of just a few." The "fundi" part of the word refers to the Earth, and "lati" refers to something like "lateral" and "moving off."

We focused a lot on the story about King Ahab and a peasant named Naboth (1 Kings 21). Ahab and other Israeli kings were known to take control of land that had been used for subsistence farming, move the peasants off, and put in an olive orchard or grape vineyard with the idea of marketing the olives and wine to trade for material for war. So indeed, a person could wonder if much has changed since then with powerful governments shifting land away from subsistence purposes and using it for war purposes—or enacting farm policies that favor unsustainable practices for the benefit of corporations.

Farmland Transfer and Why It's Important

Farm Transfer Planning: The Soft Issues Are the Hard Issues *by Kathryn Z. Ruhf*

Legacy: something handed down or received from an ancestor or predecessor. A legacy can be money or property; it can be values such as tolerance or stewardship. For farmers, a meaningful legacy typically is a rich mix of "things" and values—land, a home, equipment, relationships, farming practices, and beliefs about hard work, conservation, or innovation, for example.

Farm succession or transfer planning is as much about values, beliefs, and relationships as it is about taxes, wills, and business entities. With the average age of U.S. farmers at fifty-eight, and five times as many farmers over sixty-five as under thirty-five years old,[1] much more attention needs to be paid to farm entry and exit. Beginning farmers report that access to land is among their top challenges,[2] while in one Iowa study of retiring farmers, *two-thirds* had no identified successor.[3]

A prosperous and resilient food and farming system for our nation requires that a new generation of farmers—whether or not they come from farm backgrounds—be able to start and successfully grow farms and ranches. And if older farmers can't easily exit from farming, their land can't become available to entering farmers. And seniors' holdings are significant.

About 10 percent of all farmland is expected to change hands within the next five years alone, according to the U.S. Department of Agriculture (USDA).[4] Of the 2.1 million principal farm operators—defined as the person responsible for the day-to-day operation of the farm or ranch—farmers over the age of sixty-five account for 33 percent, and they manage about one-third of all land in farms. They own nearly 625.5 million acres of land in farms, of which about 70 million acres are rented to others.[5]

There are another 283.4 million acres rented for agriculture by landlords who are *not farmers*. Together, over *2.1 million landlords* rent farmland. Their average age is 66.5—*older* than the average farmer! This sector is comprised of retired farmers, farm widows and heirs, and other owners of agricultural property.[6]

How these lands will be transferred should be of utmost concern—not only to the families directly impacted but also to the communities that benefit from those farms and ranches, and to our society as a whole. The security of our food and farming system largely depends on the ability of farm and ranch operations to keep their farms viable, available, and affordable for the next generation, whether or not from the same family. Older farmers seek a meaningful legacy and deserve a comfortable retirement. "[Retiring farmers'] succession decisions and retirement plans are of considerable importance to the farming community and the future structure of agriculture. Continuity of the family farm and the family farm sector is highly dependent on successful transfer."[7]

Given the importance of farm transfer, it is crucial to help farmers address the issues and adequately plan. Contemporary conditions compel more attention to farm transfer planning and more support for farmers who seek a secure exit from active farming and a meaningful legacy.

Why? Because traditional methods of farm transfer are no longer sufficient to address today's agriculture. As mentioned, fewer farmers are starting out on family land. The cost of acquisition through purchase has skyrocketed in many parts of the country, making land-ownership a distant dream. In parallel, the cost of retirement often means selling farm assets for more than an entering farmer could afford, or dismantling the farm. Gradual transfers, more secure leases, mentorships, conservation easements, creative limited development, and innovative financing, for example, are methods to make transfers more viable for both entering and exiting farmers.

Notably, there is no overarching public policy on land access, tenure, and transfer. A 2010 research report states that "U.S. agriculture faces significant challenges regarding how farms and ranches are acquired, held, transferred and managed for conservation." It recommends that "public policies should encourage and support the timely transfer of farm businesses and properties in ways that assure a comfortable transition and meaningful legacy for the retiring farmer and affordable opportunity for the next generation."[8]

The USDA is paying attention. In early 2015, its Advisory Committee on Beginning Farmers and Ranchers was charged by USDA secretary Tom Vilsack to establish a subcommittee on land tenure. The subcommittee was charged with providing recommendations to the secretary on land tenure, access to land, and farm business transitions. A report was submitted with a substantial list of recommended policies, from changes in Farm Bill programs to changes in the Internal Revenue Code—all aimed at improving the conditions for agricultural land access and farm operation transfer. The likelihood of these policies being adopted as laws or regulations is unclear.

KEY TERMS AND ISSUES IN FARMLAND TRANSFER

Succession is the process of passing a business from one generation or owner to another. Sometimes succession implies a transfer within a family, but that isn't necessarily the case. For some, succession is seen as a set of social decisions, whereas transfer focuses more on the legal and economic aspects. The terms *succession, transfer,* and *transition* are often used synonymously.

Succession *planning* is just that—a plan for how a business will continue after the senior/leader exits. The plan determines who next will take leadership and/or ownership and how that transition happens. Succession issues are not unique to farm businesses, but agriculture poses unique challenges.

In agriculture, transfers can be more complex than in other business sectors. This is in part because a transfer typically considers both the land and the business. The land is often the most significant asset, and the business operator typically lives there. Many family-owned businesses have meaningful histories and assets, but farms hold unique places in the hearts of their owners, sometimes for generations. Farm businesses may transfer to a nonfamily successor, but the land may stay in the family. Conversely, the transfer of land does not equate to the transfer of a farm business. The land has unique standing, not just because of its monetary value but also because of its nonmonetary legacy.

Succession planning consists of the transfer of income, assets, and management. It involves estate planning, retirement planning, land-use planning, and business planning. Often, management is the most challenging and least attended to aspect of the transfer. How can the older generation be supported to engage in timely succession planning and exit?

What is *retirement*? The issue of aging farmers was first raised nearly fifty years ago. However, the predicted mass retirements never happened. Instead, older farmers continue to farm at ever-increasing ages, and are quitting at slower rates. This has enormous implications for farm transfers. If the senior farmer does not exit or transfer control in a timely and thoughtfully managed way, the next in line—if there is one—is much less prepared to take over, and often is discouraged from even trying.

Retirement means different things to different people. In the non-farming sector, many people "retire" the day they leave their job, period. In agriculture, older farmers stay in farming for various reasons such as greater longevity and better health. Mechanization results in less physically strenuous labor; if the farmer can still climb on the tractor, he can still farm. And while farmers may complain, most experience a strong attachment to and continuing satisfaction with at least some aspects of farming. This is part of their legacy! One farmer may say he's retired, but continues to run the combine or help with harvesting hay or pumpkins. Others may claim to be partly retired but still control the checkbook. One-quarter of surveyed Iowa farmers said they never intend to retire;[9] this is probably similar in other states. So what does that mean for the transfer and future of the operation?

If retirement is defined as providing *no managerial control or labor* to the farm, it's not hard to see why there are shades of gray. In fact, retirement is a process that can take years, and unfolds according to the unique needs and preferences of the farmer and significant others.

What are the issues? Because of the many challenges involved in succession, it's not surprising that so few farmers have adequately prepared to exit from farming. Only one-fifth of family farms survive the transfer to the next generation. "This could be attributable to the failure to develop a succession plan."[10] According to one study, only 36 percent of farmers and farmland owners have an estate plan. Eighty-two percent did not have an exit strategy, and 88 percent indicated they do not have financial plans for their retirement.[11]

The challenges are both technical and nontechnical. In fact, farm succession planning advisers quip that "the soft issues are the hard issues." The lines between the farm business and family often are blurred. Business and family goals can be hard to separate. Family communications can be fraught. Farm families—like other families—tend to avoid difficult issues and conflict. Most of us are reluctant to deal with issues like taxes, diminishment, death, and tensions with in-laws, for example. Nearly half of farmers surveyed in 2006 said they had not discussed retirement with anyone.[12] Relinquishing control, being "fair," health concerns, and changes in lifestyle, for example, can be challenging to address in family settings. The odds of success can be improved with the assistance of "outsiders" such as a family friend, trusted adviser, or professional coach.

The foundation of successful succession planning is built with a shared vision, clear goals, and open communications. Resolving financial, tax, and legal matters and management transfer are the substance. Is the operation healthy enough to transfer? Can the business accommodate two families? What changes are needed? What are the retirement income needs of the exiting farmer or farm couple, and can those needs be accommodated while enabling an affordable transition to the next farmer? How and when will decision making and control shift?

Historically, inheritance has been the most common way to acquire a farm in the United States. However, since the 1990s this traditional model of farm transfer—from older to younger generation within a family—accounts for less than half of farm acquisition. Therefore, new methods must evolve to facilitate successful transfers, especially between unrelated parties.

In fact, farmers without identified successors have particular challenges in realizing their desired legacy. In focus groups of this sector conducted in 2015,[13] farmers universally said they want to see their land stay in farming. They are open and willing to pass their operation to a nonfamily member, but they need support to develop a realistic plan and to recruit a successor. With the recent surge in interest in farming, more young and not-so-young people are entering farming. Most of them do not come from farms, and many have experience and resources. Nonetheless, their land access challenges are formidable. Improving the ways to connect those seeking farms with those seeking successors will be a significant contribution to future food and farm security.

What *services* are available to help? Some groups and institutions have well-established programs to assist and educate farm families about succession planning. More are emerging. These include so-called farm link services, succession technical assistance, and land access programs. Yet nationally, there is not yet a sufficient network of informed advisers to help farm families navigate the complexities of transition planning. We need more technical experts such as attorneys and farm financial planners, along with coaches and facilitators, retirement and health care specialists, and land planners and conservation professionals with expertise in agriculture. Farm transfer planning takes a team. And there are costs involved, costs that vary widely. Research conducted in 2011 showed that older farmers see the value of succession planning and do not consider the cost of such as an impediment.[14]

Yet it's hard to get senior farmers to engage in timely planning. The farmers in this study said that assuring the future of their land was at least as important as the future of the farmer himself. Farmers deserve a secure exit from farming, and new farmers deserve the opportunity to start and grow businesses. That's what a farm legacy is all about. The stories in this book attest to the importance of farmland owners' views of their legacy and to the possibility of realizing their vision.

Kathryn Z. Ruhf is the senior program director of the New Hampshire based nonprofit organization Land for Good.

Belonging *by John Gilbert, Iowa Falls, Iowa*

Our late parents took great pains and the time to ensure the survival of both our farm and our family bonds. It was not easy for them. Dad was fanatical about how he wanted things, but when it came right down to signing the necessary legal papers, he and Mother needed encouragement. Was it an admission of their mortality or feeling like they were relinquishing control that made them hesitate? I don't know. What I do know is the process took time, both to create and for it to work.

We were very fortunate that Dad lived till ninety-six. We know how lucky we are because his passing barely created a ripple in the farm's operation. His plan not only worked but provided the framework for us to continue the transition process to the next generation.

Our (personal and collective) relationship with *the land* may be one reason farm transition is so difficult. Suicides happened during the farm crisis when a farmer lost the *family farm*. The loss of a farm was invariably referred to as like the loss of a family member.

Is farmland transition difficult because *our land* has been in *our family* for *generations*? Or is it that everyone in the family knows the sacrifices made to pay for it during tough times? Is it the familiarity that comes from years of working the same ground, knowing intimately its foibles and eccentricities? Is it that we really understand on some primal level that we really are only caretakers ... keepers of the Holy Grail? I suspect it is all of these and more.

There is another possibility not often considered. Our attachment to a farm is because we "belong" to the land. Without belaboring the point, is farmland a case of a psychological connection that the family farm is where we "belong"?

Properties often are known by the families that own them, or the families who owned them generations back, even after all signs of a farmstead are bulldozed and buried. As tenants, there is no *sense of ownership*, but, more important, there is no sense of *belonging* to the rented farm. As more and more acres are rented, I fear the connection of *belonging* is being lost. The issue of belonging is due more attention, because it probably is what separates farmland from other real estate. And it is probably what smacks farmers as being wrong when absentee owners see land as an "investment" (whether purchased or inherited).

So, just what does *belonging* mean? Is it like belonging to a particular church, or being a fan of a certain sports team? Is it like being a member of a certain class or other group tied by proximity? Or is it on a philosophical—if not spiritual—level? I don't know. By reading Aldo Leopold or Wendell Berry or any of those who've touched on this, we get a feel for what our connection involves. It may be enough to just understand we have the connection.

The takeaway of being a landowner is we have responsibilities to care for it, use it wisely, and pass it along to someone who will continue the stewardship. Finding a good transition plan is complicated, but it is our opportunity to ensure our land is cared for in the manner we feel is best, even from the grave.

The proverbial first step is the hardest and most important.

The Ladder to Farmland Ownership
by Michael Duffy and Teresa Opheim

Michael Duffy with Maria Rosmann of Rosmann Family Farms in Harlan, Iowa.

Michael Duffy, professor emeritus of economics from Iowa State University, is well known for, among other research, his surveys on Iowa farmland values. He visited the Practical Farmers offices to discuss a variety of farmland ownership issues with editor Teresa Opheim.

TO: This book focuses on the transitions taking place with *farmland* but not with *farm business* transfer, which raises so many other issues....

MD: People have such emotional ties to the land, so your focus is a valid one. Family farms are businesses in which the land is the bulk of the operation's value. This makes farmland transfer such a difficult area to navigate.

TO: A while back, I asked beginning farmers who are members of Practical Farmers how important it was that they eventually own land. Responses were varied, but here's one: "Though not necessary, or even desirable at first, landownership must eventually be part of the package of farming so a farmer can put up buildings and infrastructure to support production, and build equity in an appreciating long-term asset." I've heard you talk about the "land tenure ladder." Would you explain what that is?

MD: The "land tenure ladder" was written down in the 1920s, and it is still relevant today. The ladder includes rungs like being an unpaid laborer on your parents' home farm, being a "hired man," spending time as a tenant operator, becoming a mortgaged owner and then a full owner. Not everyone steps on every rung, of course, but you get the idea.

As young people start off working, they build up capital, and they can borrow a little money and work up the ladder to ownership. Too many young people today want to start at the top of the ladder.

TO: And too many older farmers are not stepping away and letting the next generation take over.

MD: We've made it easier to farm and easier to farm longer because we've substituted capital (such as sophisticated equipment and chemicals) for labor. I know of one case where the farmer was ninety-four, and he had identified a successor—who was seventy-two! Many farmers don't have a successor identified and have not gone through the planning and hard work of farm business transfer.

TO: At Practical Farmers, many of the farmland owners I have talked with plan to divide their farmland equally among their farming and nonfarming heirs. Is this common in the U.S.?

MD: Much research shows that farmland owners intend to transfer the land equally to their heirs. It's been that way for a while in this country.

TO: This often puts the farming heir at a disadvantage. The farming heir has put a lifetime of work into the farm, not to mention lived close by and often been the one to help Mom and Dad through the years. On the other hand, there is the question about who was asked to farm in the first place. In the words of one female member of Practical Farmers: "It was always assumed my brother would farm. No one ever even asked me if I was interested."

MD: We have a female friend who had two brothers. The brothers were given all the farmland, because the assumption was that her husband would take care of her. Both of the brothers died, and now the land is out of the family. And our friend is the one taking care of her mother.

TO: Many of these farmland owners who want to give their heirs an inheritance of equal economic value often want the farming heir to continue to farm the family land as well. Can they really accomplish both goals?

MD: You cannot maximize more than one variable. You have to prioritize. Most people aren't going to have the resources to do both. It becomes so important to consider the various goals and decide "this is my number one goal." When you have both farming and nonfarming heirs, equal may not be fair.

TO: What do you mean by that?

MD: If you have a child who spends his or her career working the farm and helping take care of Mom, shouldn't there be additional value in that? The responsibility of taking care of the mother should be recognized. The responsibility of having built the farming operation should be recognized. Equal and fair may not be the same thing. If I want my child to continue to farm, I will give him more because I want to see the farm continued. That's why you need to decide what your goals are and prioritize your goals.

We need to present alternatives on how a farmland owner with farming and nonfarming heirs can recognize the financial value of the child who has stayed home to farm. The use of life insurance can help. So can an approach where the farming child gradually buys out the nonfarming siblings. All of this requires advanced planning.

TO: And a lot of communication among family members.

MD: If you don't communicate, you set yourself up for all kinds of problems.

TO: Good family communication is easier said than done, though. The things that are the most important are sometimes the hardest to talk about.

MD: No one wants to think about their mortality. Or they say, "I don't care what happens, I will be dead." Well that's a hell of a way to think about it. Some farmers may not want their business to continue. "I don't want my kids to go through what I did, so I will just give them the land asset," they say. We saw a lot of that attitude in the late 1980s, when everyone was so pessimistic about farming.

By the way, we did a survey of small nonfarming businesses a while back, and the results weren't much different. Many of them didn't have successors for their businesses either.

TO: Well, there is no shortage of people wanting to farm now.

MD: And many of them are going to have to get creative about how they generate income, such as with value-added enterprises. I talked to a guy a while back who said his view of sustainable agriculture was to grow a feed crop, a food crop, and a cash crop. Like the Rosmanns near Harlan, where they have a variety of crop and livestock enterprises that complement each other. And they have enterprises such as Maria's farm store as well.

TO: A great example. Ron and Maria Rosmann now have sons and a daughter-in-law working with them, so three families are employed on 700 acres. And I know PFI people who have more children back on fewer acres. They are not getting rich, but they are supporting themselves.

MD: The Rosmanns and others like them are putting a lot of management expertise and labor into their operations. They work hard.

TO: There is no shortage of people interested in "impact investing," where they want a financial return but want to advance a social good as well. What is the role being played by nonfarming investors in the farmland area? It seems that a lot of beginning farmers need those partnerships with nonfarmers, especially if they want to eventually own land.

MD: That's the land tenure ladder! Beginning farmers need that expertise and financial help. There is a lot of negative talk about nonfarmer investors and non-operator farmland owners. There is an assumption that they won't take care of the land, but I don't know if that is a valid assumption. A lot of them used to farm. A lot of them are widows—10 percent of the land in Iowa is owned by single women over seventy-five. It is not likely that most of these women are farming at that age, so that's 10 percent of Iowa's land that could be available for a younger person getting started.

By the way, Iowa's farmland owners can earn a tax credit for leasing land to a beginning farmer. That should be a federal program as well. Another policy solution would be to forgive capital gains taxes if you sell to a beginning farmer. When you sell your house, the first $250,000 in capital gains is forgiven, so you don't have to pay income tax on that amount. If I sold you my farm and the first $1 million in capital gains was forgiven, that might make the land move faster.

TO: In his Farm Legacy Letter, farmer Jeff Klinge has written that "high land prices are only good for somebody who's using farmland as an investment to make money and not for the people who are actually trying to make a living farming it."

MD: There are very few periods where land hasn't been high-priced, because people look at land as a source of wealth. We complain about high land prices, but we don't complain about high income. Why is land high-priced? Because you can make a good living off of it. If income is high, land values are high.

TO: That's true if you are growing commodities like corn and soybeans.

MD: We have placed virtually all of our focus on corn and soybeans in Iowa. Our research dollars too. Now the universities don't have as much public money, but there are companies that want the corn and beans to keep going, so they support that. But what can we do about it?

TO: What about the vegetable farmer who wants or needs to farm in a rapidly urbanizing area?

MD: All bets are off in urbanizing areas. Land is always valued at the "highest and best use," which is considered putting houses on it. In the Midwest, farmland preservation laws have not been as popular as in other parts of the country. We are still considered pretty wide open here. And remember that for a farmer needing retirement income, selling land located in an urbanizing area may be very much welcomed.

TO: Let's get back to goals. It seems simple and obvious, but worth repeating. Too often farmland owners haven't thought enough about what they want most for the future of their farmland. We talked about two common goals: to provide land for a farming heir to farm, and to provide an inheritance of equal economic value. Farmland owners' goals could also include benefiting a charity or helping a beginning farmer get started, for example. What matters may not mean maximizing financial return. For PFI leaders and farmers Tom and Irene Frantzen, a top goal is stemming the tide of land consolidation. According to the Frantzens, the concentration of landownership they see is disrupting rural communities and a threat to democracy.

MD: The big question: Are we going to continue to see land consolidation because of our focus on cheap food? If we continue to move in that direction, the majority of our land will be farmed by big operations. We will continue to see midsize farms disappear. And that will exacerbate problems. But we also are seeing more and more consumer interest and concern with how our food is raised. And a lot of creativity in responding to that and adding value on the farm.

Putting *Map of My Kingdom* on the Map

by Mary Swander

I sat across the desk from Teresa Opheim, then–executive director of Practical Farmers of Iowa. She had asked to meet with me in her downtown office on a cold, snowy January day in Ames, Iowa.

"Would you write a play for PFI about farmland transfer?" she asked.

What an interesting assignment, I thought. I had had my own experience with farmland transitions, having inherited the family farm with my two brothers at age twenty-three. I knew how contentious the subject could be for all involved, and I knew how farmland transfer could shape the agricultural landscape.

In the last few decades, one family farm after another had become folded into larger operations. I also knew that farmland transition was a huge issue in our times, with a lot of U.S. farmland set to change hands in the coming years.

My playwriting seed cap began to spin. How would I make this play dynamic? How would I avoid cliché? How would I make the show flexible, easy to tour, and reasonably priced? I didn't want anything stock. I didn't want to assemble a symbolic farm family around their kitchen table to let them fight out the issue. That scenario had played out too many times, and it involved a relatively large cast. Every actor included in a play costs money. The greater the number of actors in the script, the greater the headaches with scheduling. How would I open up the script to a more panoramic view of the issue? Of not only the families but also the lawyers, the accountants, and the bankers involved?

Teresa sent me off with a list of PFI farmers to interview about their individual farmland transfer issues. I jumped in my car with my graduate student assistant Zachary Hawkins, and we drove the countryside, the back roads still frozen and slick. We spoke with large farmers and small. We spoke with those farmers who had made smooth transitions, and with those who had become stuck in decades-long conflicts with family members.

On the way home from these farms, Zachary and I discussed what we'd heard, what new information we'd gained, what insights we'd gleaned. We began to realize that each family's situation was unique and could present distinct problems. Yet some common archetypal, even biblical, scenarios did emerge. The Cain and Abel story repeated itself—one family member coming to blows with another over their piece of land. The return of the prodigal son story also came up again and again—a relative returning to the farm after a long estrangement or absence, only to try to claim his inheritance.

The stories piled up. But I still struggled to find the structure of the play. Who would become my fictional main characters? What kind of set would frame the action? What was the main conflict? I'd eliminated the symbolic farm-family-at-their-kitchen-table scenario, but what would replace it?

Then it was time for the Practical Farmers conference in Ames, where several knowledgeable farmers were to give a workshop on farmland transition.

"We need to go to this," I told Zach, "and look for possibilities for main characters and conflict."

Longtime PFI member Michael Rosmann was one of the seminar speakers. Rosmann is a mediator, an author, and a psychologist who had once been in academe, only to return to his family farm in Harlan, Iowa, to work with families who were going through farmland transition. Both Zach and I immediately saw a mediator as a main character for the play. And then the play's conflict became clear. The show would be about how this mediator navigated families through their negotiations and estate planning. Positive farmland transfers are possible, not always, not every time, but given some thought, preparation, and skill, farmland transfers could produce happy endings.

A few weeks later, Zach and I found ourselves facing Rosmann across his desk in his office on his farm. A large man with a booming voice behind an equally large desk, Rosmann graciously spent a good part of a day with us, providing insights, expertise, and best- and worst-case scenarios about farmland transfer. He gave us a psychologist's view of the agrarian character, the many trials facing a farmer, and how an individual may meet those challenges. A founder of Agri-Wellness, he has been a longtime advocate for the behavioral health care of the agricultural population.

"I saw the suicide rate of farmers climbing," Rosmann said, "and I thought, my God, someone has to help these people."

Sobered, but at the same time heartened to find such knowledge and understanding, I drove home recognizing the complexity of the role of the land mediator. The next day I began making sketches in my notebook. How about a one-woman show? My main character, a land mediator, needed to be highly intelligent, with an in-depth knowledge of not only psychology, law, and estate planning but of agronomy and rural sociology. The fictionalizing process began.

Women own almost 50 percent of all the farmland in Iowa. In my family, the century farm passed down through three generations of women, and I knew well the barriers that all of us faced with farming. I decided a woman land mediator would take the stage to help depict the female side of the issue. She needed to be credible, well-credentialed. I gave her both a Ph.D. and a J.D. Who could top that? I saw her as a strong woman, tough, but bringing grace to difficult situations. I called her Angela.

So now Zach, the fictional Angela, and I drove the countryside, talking to more farmers, bankers, and lawyers about farmland transfer. We spoke to families surrounded by urban sprawl, with farmers who had no offspring who wanted to farm, with farmers who had three or four offspring who all wanted to work the land. The combinations were endless. We spoke with bankers who spoke of the reasons farmers are reticent to discuss finances with their families. We spoke to lawyers who strove to understand the emotional value most families put on the land.

Zach dove into the library archives and retrieved newspaper articles of a famous Iowa land dispute case that ended in murder. I read the pile of articles with the same sadness and shock that had overcome me when I'd read the same original articles in the *Des Moines Register* years ago.

I researched agriculture in ancient times. I researched the history of agricultural land transfer in the United States and the different programs that various states were using to help farms transition. Again, each state had to address different kinds of pressures upon the land, from soaring land values to depopulation.

Finally, summer arrived and I stationed myself in my little writing studio on my acreage near Kalona, Iowa. The ceiling fan spun over my head, the horses and goats nibbled the grass at the gate, and the swallowtail butterflies flitted casually over my garden. There was nothing casual about my writing habits, though. I was teaching full time and had precious little time to write during the academic year, so summer was my time to complete major projects. I'd mapped out the month of July for this farmland transition play.

Every day I entered my cabin and holed up with my laptop. I let nothing disturb me. I wanted the play to be grounded in local reality but to have universal themes and literary allusions. I wanted the play to work on several different levels. I wanted farmers and ordinary people to be able to relate to the language, ideas, and themes, but at the same time, I wanted to write a work of art that had a literary context. I thought about all the works of literature that I could recall that had land transfer issues at their core.

I drove to the public library in town and borrowed copies of the Old and New Testaments, the Koran, Willa Cather's *My Ántonia*, Shakespeare's *King Lear*, and Jane Smiley's *A Thousand Acres*. While in town, I ran some errands, and everywhere I went—to the hardware store, to the general store, to the bank—every clerk wanted to know what I was writing this summer. When I told them that I was writing about farmland transfer, I needed to go no further. Each and every one of the clerks had a personal story—some good, some bad, some ugly. I no longer needed to drive hundreds of miles to interview folks about farmland transfer. Folks were now stepping forward, approaching me with their tales.

I toted my books home and spent a week behind my closed cabin door rereading the texts and taking notes. I developed a rough outline of the play, drafting a series of scenes. Then I put the outline, all the notes, and all the interview transcriptions away and began to do the actual writing. I let the character of Angela Martin begin to take shape, find her own voice, become her own person. I drew her personal story from my own, incorporating my own grandmother's land transfer decision into the opening scene. My grandmother Nellie became Angela's grandmother Millie. My family's struggles to hold on to their land and eke out a living in Ireland became Angela's family narrative:

> *The ancestral farm was 80 acres, but pure rock—only 20 acres were actually tillable. And that soil—that 20 acres of arable turf—they cut that up for fuel and literally burnt through all their farmland. So the farmers went down to the ocean, hauled up these large baskets of seaweed and kelp from the beach, and laid it across the rocks and the barren scars. After years and years of composting what they were pulling out of the ocean, that soil became tillable.*
>
> *And when my ancestors came here, they actually had great soil, but they burnt through it just the same. And when the Dust Bowl came ... well, there wasn't a lot of seaweed here.*

Then the scenarios from my research began to fold into the script, moving fluently from one situation to another. I gave Angela the challenging acting job of taking on the roles of about twenty different people. I opened the gate to the religious and literary material, and they found their way into the play. By the time I'd been in my cabin about three weeks, I was heading toward a new understanding of farmland transfer. The issue became more than just squabbling families and disappearing family farms. I began asking the questions: Can we actually own land, a part of the earth? To whom does it really belong? What about this notion of private property?

The concept of private property reeled my mind back through the socioeconomic systems of Western civilization, from feudalism to Marxism. I preferred to look toward a different philosophy. I drove back to the library and looked at Native American texts and their concept of Mother Earth.

> *"What is this you call property?" Massasoit asked the early settlers of Plymouth Colony. "It cannot be the earth, for the land is our mother, nourishing all her children, beasts, birds, fish and all men. The woods, the streams, everything on it belongs to everybody and is for the use of all. How can one man say it belongs only to him?"*

I ended up with a sense of the sacred in connection to the land. No matter what worldview we hold of the land, no matter what economic system we embrace, we are dealing with land that provides us food, that sustains us, that has a resonance of its own. Farmland is not just another asset like a stock or bond. Those of us who are lucky enough to "own" this natural resource—at least for "a little while," as Willa Cather says—have an obligation to tend it well and pass it on to the next generation with care, to be stewards of the earth.

Toward the end of the play, one of Angela Martin's clients relates how she and her husband were influenced by Pope John Paul II's visit to Iowa and his directive to preserve the land. The wife went to see the pope live, and the husband listened to his speech on the radio at home, but the words of the Holy Father sparked both of them to not only work hard to improve the natural environment of their farm, but to take some real time and effort to find their way toward a smooth farmland transfer with their children:

> And the pope started to talk and I was looking around at all these people and Gerry must have been milking, not really listening much, and then suddenly we heard the pope talking about the need to be stewards of the land and how we are called to leave the Earth, the soil in better condition than we found it. . . . "The land is yours to preserve from generation to generation." That hit me. And it hit Gerry.

By August I had a script called *Map of My Kingdom*, the title taken from King Lear:

> Meantime we shall express our darker purpose.
> Give me the map there. Know that we have divided
> In three our kingdom: and 'tis our fast intent
> To shake all cares and business from our age;
> Conferring them on younger strengths, while we
> Unburthen'd crawl toward death.

Then the long editing and revision process began. I then turned the script over to Matt Foss, the director and dramaturge. Foss brought a special brilliance and creative zeal to the script. He trimmed away more chunks from the manuscript and smoothed out the narrative transitions and voice. He helped tie together the anecdotes and metaphors. We sat together in a coffee shop and went over the changes, and developed other passages. We passed the manuscript back and forth and back forth, nipping and tucking.

Foss was working on another show, an adaptation of Upton Sinclair's *The Jungle* at the Oracle Theatre in Chicago. So Elizabeth Thompson, the award-winning actor who would debut *Map of My Kingdom* in Iowa, drove to Chicago where Foss rehearsed her performance between rehearsals of *The Jungle*. Thompson had been one of Foss's students at Iowa State University and had starred in many theater productions throughout her college career.

Finally, we were ready for the debut at the Scattergood School Meeting House near West Branch, Iowa, in the summer of 2014. On a hot, humid night in mid-July, Teresa Opheim, PFI board members, sponsors, farmers, and others gathered for a meal in the school cafeteria when the sky let loose with lightning and a downpour of rain. Near showtime, we darted through the wind and torrents to the meetinghouse, drenched and disheveled, to squeeze together on the wooden benches.

"We're under a tornado watch," Opheim said. "So note the exits in this room. Should a storm approach, you need to go to the basement of the main building. That serves as a shelter."

Lightning cracked. Thunder boomed. Rain gushed against the windows of the historic meetinghouse. But the show went on. All the sound effects provided an ironic and fitting backdrop to *Map of My Kingdom*, a play that alludes to King Lear, the man who descended into madness in a violent storm over the transfer of his land to his daughters. Elizabeth Thompson had a mastery of the language of the play, moving about the stage with a dancer's grace and poise, seamlessly transitioning from scene to scene, from character to character. One moment she was in the voice of King Lear, the next in the voice of Grandma Millie telling a joke about a farmer in his field confronting a minister who had stopped to attempt a conversion.

"Are you laboring in the vineyard of the Lord, my good man?" the minister asked. And the farmer, he looks at the preacher, he looks at the field. . . . "Naw, these are soybeans."

When the show was over, I conducted a talk-back on the play. The expertise in the room was phenomenal, with almost everyone present having had to wrestle with the topic at one time or another in their

Tom and Irene Frantzen lead the discussion following a performance of Map of My Kingdom *at the Blazek Barn near Lawler, Iowa.*

lives. The conversation was lively, moving from personal anecdotes to larger philosophical views. This gathering also recognized the urgency of the issue. They looked upon the play as a vehicle to start the conversation among landowners—not to preach or even to teach, but to let the audience members begin to contemplate their goals for their land, then open the dialogue with their families.

At the end of the evening, Tom Frantzen, a longtime, pioneering Practical Farmers of Iowa member and sustainable farmer from northeast Iowa, asked everyone to go home to their communities and set up a performance of *Map of My Kingdom*.

More performances followed. An old freight house in Chariton. A beautiful Lutheran church in Decorah. The state-of-the-art Wilson Performing Arts Center in Red Oak. Then: the Grinnell Area Arts Council, the Perry Carnegie Library Museum, Living History Farms in Des Moines. We did a show at the PFI Conference in January to our biggest audience of over 300 people. Then the PFI board, staff, and other members revved into gear and began to book shows in their local communities. Relatives of the cast also began to help. Shows in Lytton, Charles City, Orange City, and Storm Lake followed.

At the conclusion of one performance, we had an audience member in the first row jump to her feet and announce, "My family is going through transfer right now and it's just awful. We're fighting all the time. Mom is exhausted. My brother won't talk to me. We need help. Is there someone in the audience who can help?"

We organized panels of experts to discuss the issue after the performances: lawyers and estate planners, accountants, extension agents, and ministers. The lawyers mapped out various legal options for farmland transfer. The accountants urged farmers to assemble their team of experts and have them all work together. The extension agents had a wealth of free information, websites, and other materials to help farmers. And the ministers asked farmers to break through their denial and address the issue while they were still in good health. "Farmland transfer always comes up at the funeral," one minister said. "And it can cause chaos for a family."

Teresa Opheim stepped in to try and back up the follow-up discussion from a focus on strategies (such as putting land in a trust) to a focus on deciding what farmland owners want most for the future of their farmland. What is a family's top goal? An on-farm family member continuing the work on the land? To provide income for future generations? To benefit a charity? The potential goals were so many, the number of farmland owners who had carefully thought through their goals far fewer.

More shows followed, from Maquoketa, Cedar Falls, Fort Dodge, Washington, and more. Requests started coming in from out of state. We performed at the Federal Reserve Bank in Chicago and at the University of Massachusetts—significant venues. On the local level, *Map of My Kingdom* was fulfilling my vision for rural theater: entertainment that raised key rural issues and strengthened a sense of community. In addition, it was showing off spectacular Iowa venues, from the DeWitt Opera House to the Blazek Barn near Lawler to Chase the Adventure Lodge in Decorah.

As I continued to respond to the demand for shows, we also moved on plans for a video based on the play. On the opposite side of the state, Joe Hubers, an award-winning filmmaker of Passenger Productions from Sioux Falls, South Dakota, set up shop at Northwestern College in Orange City, Iowa. Hubers gathered director Matt Foss, actor Cora Vander Broek, and me to Orange City, where he transformed the stage play into an audio-visual wonder. Hubers, Foss, and Vander Broek were all graduates of Northwestern College, so a warm and supportive live audience composed of relatives, former professors, and interested townspeople filled the seats of the DeWitt Theatre Arts Center. Many in the audience were seeing *Map of My Kingdom* for the second, third, or fourth time.

So, video in hand, how will *Map of My Kingdom* proceed? The show keeps touring and is spreading out beyond the Iowa borders. There are countless ways the play and video may be used for educational purposes. The farmland transfer issue is still urgent and is growing more so every day. If I ever doubt that *Map of My Kingdom* is effective, I simply think back to the day that I was invited into a rural church basement in northeast Iowa to have coffee with eight widows pondering their transfer situations.

All the women owned their family farms. All were struggling with how to pass on the property to their children, how to be fair, how to be equal, how to maintain the integrity of their farms, the land that they'd lived on most of their adult lives, the land that they loved. One woman's husband had died without a will. Another feared that she would become a burden on her own family, the farm having to be sold to pay for nursing home costs. All were gathering their teams of experts and pondering all the options, what can be a confusing array of choices.

"We come and go, but the land is always here," Willa Cather wrote in *O Pioneers!* And Angela Martin hangs on to these words and this idea in *Map of My Kingdom*, repeating the literary passage to give herself perspective through her career of dealing with the land. "And the people who love it and understand it, are the people who own it—for a little while."

It's a tough conversation, Martin concludes, on how we end our "little while" with the land and let someone else's "little while" start.

We only have that little sliver of time to make sure that that land keeps getting loved, keeps getting understood, one "while" after another.

Anyone interested in a Map of My Kingdom *performance should contact Mary Swander: mary.swander@yahoo.com or 319-683-2613. Complete information about the play can be found on her website: http:// www.maryswander.com.*

The Bounty of the Lord
by Tom and Irene Frantzen, New Hampton, Iowa

As Chickasaw County, Iowa, farmers Tom and Irene Frantzen hit their late fifties, they began thinking seriously about their farm's legacy. The Frantzens are followers of Holistic Management, which they used as the driver as they worked out the details of their generational transfer. As Tom says, "The basic principle in Holistic Management is that we have no idea where we're going if we don't have goals."

After years of work, Tom and Irene came to a momentous decision: Upon their deaths, their farm will be transferred to Practical Farmers of Iowa, the 320 acres to be kept together generation after generation. Their farming son, James, will be the preferred tenant. An accompanying governing agreement specifies that the farm will not be sold or mortgaged, sustainable farming practices will be maintained, and the Frantzen Farm name will be preserved.

Generational transfer goal: long-term protection for a true Iowa family farm that has significant conservation features blended into a working landscape.

Farm motto: I shall see the bounty of the Lord in the land of the living (from Psalm 27:13).

TOM FRANTZEN

We needed a strategy that allows the farm to survive a variety of tragedies and unexpected results, or we really don't have a plan for the future. What if something would happen to James? Then it would end as far as it being the *Frantzen Farm*. He could die in a car accident, he could become disabled or have some kind of health issue that would prevent him from being able to farm. We aren't looking at just James's generation. We want the farm to be continually preserved and kept in the hands of an organization that's going to care for the land like we do and will maintain the name *Frantzen Farm*.

Now people are going to say, "Why didn't you just will the farmland to your son?" When the pope visited Iowa in 1979, he said that the land is ours to be preserved for generation upon generation. He didn't just say preserve the land for a generation. He said generation upon generation. We think that the farm is best preserved by a group than by any individual.

There are real problems today with selling our farm to our son as my father sold his farm to us. Land values are ridiculously high. Our son would end up with a real serious burden of debt, regardless of the price.

Future tenants, family or nonfamily, should have a basis for a profitable operation. They will not be burdened with interest and principal payments on the farm. We are all tenants on our farms in our lifetimes anyway.

JAMES FRANTZEN

My parents' decision protects me long-term. If I had to purchase this farmland, I would have great debt for a number of years. That would really tie my hands from being able to improve or expand the farm. Taking that burden of farmland debt out of the picture might open up doors to other opportunities down the road....

Generational transfer is unique to every situation and every farm family. Our family is providing an example for generational transfer,

but we certainly don't foresee everyone doing this. This is what fit for us. You have to sit down as a family and discuss what's going to fit best. You have to go over multiple aspects and multiple future scenarios, whether they are economic or family-related.

IRENE FRANTZEN

To my future heirs,

I grew up living on a farm with my three sisters. My mom and dad were hard workers and always provided for us. I have fond memories of playing on the farm, always having dogs and cats for pets, fresh food from the garden, home-cooked meals that were always delicious, and much more.

Of course, there was always work to do, and we had to do our share. As I grew into my teens, I was not always happy on the farm. I had some lousy jobs, like the chicken chores, pulling weeds in the garden, cleaning house, and picking up rocks in the fields. I never got to drive the tractor or do other fun jobs on the farm. I wasn't the oldest, I wasn't the youngest, and I was not Dad's favorite. I'm sure my dad was hoping for a boy by the time I was born! I was just kind of a . . . nobody, I thought. I couldn't wait to graduate from high school and be on my own.

I swore up and down I would never marry a farmer and certainly never raise a chicken. After being on my own for a while, I met Tom. I fell in love, married this farmer in 1976, and eventually raised some chickens on a farm. They say love is blind!

The early years on the farm were a true challenge. We survived the transfer of the farm from Tom's parents to us, difficult weather conditions, and the Farm Crisis of the '80s. There were times when we questioned where we were going and how we could do better. Something was missing, and we didn't know what.

Then it happened. It was a crisp, beautiful fall day in early October that the pope came to Iowa's Living History Farms. We didn't attend, unlike so many others who did, including Tom's mother. Instead, Tom decided to paint the barn, and I was probably doing whatever in the garden or taking care of other matters. While Tom painted, he listened on the radio to the pope's message. The pope talked about being good stewards. "The land is yours to preserve from generation upon generation." It struck such a chord that Tom almost fell off the ladder. He also shared, so many times over, how he felt like the pope was right on that ladder with him, talking to him personally. The pope's message would change us forever. It was the beginning of a whole new look on our lives and the future of this 320 acres in Chickasaw County.

We then began our journey of being better stewards on the farm. We involved ourselves with the Land Stewardship Project, Practical Farmers of Iowa, and participated in Holistic Management. These groups and individuals who practiced sustainable methods helped us change our own practices. Some great things were happening on our farm. It just made sense to reduce outside inputs, such as chemicals and insecticides. We planted shelterbelts, installed a farm pond, used cover crops, brought back cattle to the farm, and diversified the farm with alternative crops. Researchers from various institutes took notice and came to our farm to study the effects of these practices on insects and animals.

We had some great experiences and shared them with others through many field days. We've been fortunate to have visitors from all but one continent. We have shared with others so many meals around the kitchen table. Every meal I have prepared—the fresh-baked goods, produce from the garden, cooking our own meats—has been a pleasure, since I enjoy cooking and baking. We've learned so much from the visitors!

As the years continued, other significant events took place that changed our farming habits. After Tom received a chemical injury, we decided to eliminate any chemical use on this farm. And so was the beginning of the farm becoming organic. I will always remember the phone call Tom made at the kitchen table to the CEO of Organic Valley CROPP Cooperative, George Siemon, asking him to start an organic pork program. As I write this letter, the Frantzen Farm is 100 percent certified organic, which includes all the crops, beef, and pork.

What we've worked so hard for over the years is truly a labor of love. I do not want anyone to destroy the natural beauty and the land-scape that means so much to this family. With that in mind, my number one goal for this farm, long after I'm gone, is to provide farmland for a true Iowa family farm (preferably family descendants) that has significant conservation features blended into a working landscape. I want the farm protected from land consolidation. I want the farm to be kept together and to keep family harmony and positive relation-ships.

We do not know what the future has in store, so Tom and I felt it best to bequeath the Frantzen Farm to Practical Farmers of Iowa. By doing this, it will always be known as the Frantzen Farm and pro-tected from any land baron. We believe this is the best gift we could ever give to our heirs. I hope that there will always be a descendant farming and living here, but if there isn't someday, at least I know it will always be cared for in a sustainable fashion with a family living here and experiencing what is all around them.

Raising my family on the farm has been one of my greatest joys. Jess, Jolene, and James helped plant the trees on the farm, baled hay, picked rocks, planted and harvested the crops, did livestock chores, and much more. Maybe they thought at the time it was a lot of work and Mom and Dad weren't being fair, just as I thought my mom and dad weren't being fair. I never realized growing up that they, too, were teaching good work ethics and appreciation for the simple pleasures all around. How fortunate our kids were to have opportunities to work with researchers on the farm that many others at their age will never experience.

I sure enjoyed the laughs along the way. I remember the pet turkeys that always entertained. The kids fed the chickens and picked the eggs. Jess still always has to have fried eggs in the morning, just like her dad. I remember the first time Jess drove a tractor. I think I bit off all my fingernails. She actually did better than I thought she would.

Jolene loved the cats on the farm. She had a name for all and carried them everywhere she went. When she wasn't playing with the cats, she would love to help me in the garden, planting and watering all the produce and flowers. James couldn't have just a sand tire; he had to have a large sand area. He played forever with his tractors and Tonkas.

The kids would fight over who had to pick up rocks in the fields. They would have disputes while building or repairing fence with their dad, and argue about which row they should be raking in the hay field. But they also had cookouts and bonfires, swam with friends at the pond, and had fun with the four-wheeler. They made good use of the clubhouse in the backyard that now houses my garden tools.

Our farm motto that we have followed for so many years says it all: "I shall see the bounty of the Lord in the land of the living" (from Psalm 27:13). I have received my bounty!! We nurtured and raised our children in no better place than on this farm. I wouldn't have changed this for all the money in the world. I have watched this farm evolve into a beautiful place called home and hope that my grandchildren and great-grandchildren will understand that someday.

There have been a lot of sweat and tears, and mistakes along the way. But the farm has provided a stable income and a good quality of life. When I think of the pope's message of preserving the land from generation upon generation, I understand why we made the changes that we did. It was our responsibility—our call—to care for and to protect this land and to have something to pass on far into the future.

After the kids were grown and gone, I found myself more involved with the daily operations of the farm. I distinctly remember one day when I was by myself picking rocks in the field across the creek west of the farmstead. I was near the edge of the field at the top of the hill where we have a windbreak of border trees to the farm. I stopped for a few minutes and sat on the grass by the trees and looked all around. I had a great view of the fields, the house, the barn, the hoop buildings, cattle in the pasture, the pond where ducks were wading and geese were in sight. The birds were chirping. I took in the fresh air, the green grass, and the daisy I had just picked. I felt like I was in true harmony with the land and finally realized what my purpose in life was that I had searched for so long ago when growing up. I was meant to be on a farm, raising a family, teaching them to appreciate the beauty all around us. I started to cry happy tears. I asked myself, how can this be so beautiful? I felt so content. I thought about what my father-in-law would say if he were still here today. I know he would be very pleased to see that we carried on to another generation of loving the land and doing a good job of farming. I also thought about what this place would look like down the road long after we are gone. Will the farm look the same? Will it have even more diversity? Will our family descendants be farming it?

I imagined our grandkids and great-grandkids running and playing and someday farming it. I thought about all the changes we've made over the years. I want to be remembered someday for caring for the land, not destroying it. I take pride we did the best we could while farming. My wish is that our children and their children will truly understand and appreciate the importance of their roots and how it all started here.

Most important, I am at peace with the choice we made for the Frantzen Farm. The day we sat around the kitchen table discussing the estate plans of the farm with our kids, with their blessings, and pushing the start button on the fax machine when we submitted our farm transfer agreement, will be forever instilled in my mind. This is the greatest gift Tom and I can give to the Frantzen family. This farm will always be protected and guided by Practical Farmers. We have taken the burdens away from our family, with hopes that it will be easier for heirs to continue to farm this land. It is an atmosphere of love and affection for all growing things . . . a beautiful place to live, with an attractive and colorful landscape that I call home.

The Frantzen Farm is a legacy of love, dedication, and perseverance. Farming to me is a form of art. Just as a paintbrush is on canvas, we've used our tools and skills to work, protect, and love the land. I hope that others in the future will treat this farm as a continued work of art in progress.

TOM FRANTZEN

My farm is 320 acres located in Chickasaw County. I have owned the farm since 1978, and my family has owned it since 1938. Enterprises on our farm include beef cows with retained calves fed out, brood sows with fed-out market hogs, corn, soybean food and feed, small grains, hay, and pasture. All are certified organic. We had dairy on the farm until 1958, and poultry until 1975. Over the years, we also became 100 percent organic and market our products through a co-op.

The farm was all wet prairie in 1880, and now it is cropland with intensive subsurface drainage. Over the years, we have added shelterbelts on much of the land to protect the streams. The wildlife is back!

My number one goal for my farmland is to stem the tide of land consolidation. This is my very top goal because our democracy is at stake if we have fewer and fewer landowners. I would give my life for our democracy.

A former Supreme Court justice said that you can have great concentration of wealth or you can have the democratic process. You cannot have both. We find the concentration of landownership and the escalation of its worth very destructive to rural communities. We find those factors a huge threat to the democratic process. We personally can't change those trends that are going on, but we don't have to be a part of them, either.

To divide up this farm and sell its assets off to the highest bidder is in complete conflict with our goals. Our children understand this. They realize that because of our generational transfer plan, they won't benefit from this current run-up in land values. They understand the love and care and the legacy of the land we are trying to preserve.

The following goals are also my priorities: Providing a place where a family can make a living. Keeping the farm together. And conserving the soil and water resources, biodiversity, and a place for wildlife and hunting.

This farm has a story that started 100 years ago. A Swiss couple, the Stauffachers, built this farm out of a tract of tall, wet prairie. The Frantzens came here dirt poor and lived and farmed here in the midst of the Great Depression. Today, our farm is profitable, and we provide sustainable employment. It is a good place to work and an important part of a rural community. It involves many other businesses in very positive ways. Down the road, maybe the Frantzen Farm will even support more families. There are no rules saying what the farm has to look like in the future. One hundred years ago, it was carved out of a chunk of tallgrass prairie, and it has been changed enormously in many different ways since.

Why Beat Your Neighbor by a Bushel?

by Jon Bakehouse, Hastings, Iowa

For twenty years now, I have been farming this land that goes up to the West Nishnabotna River one mile to the west. My great-great-grandparents moved here from Indiana in the 1880s and built this house that my wife, son, and I call home. I moved to the house in 2001 and married my wife in 2004. Our son, Anderson, was born in 2010. It is amazing to live in this three-story, twenty-room house but also a big responsibility to maintain it. While we have had to concede some of the authentic parts of the house—push-button light switches, wavy-glassed windows, and no air-conditioning, to name a few—we have tried to maintain the keyhole window, the fountain in the front yard, and as much of the original interior woodwork and finish as possible. Though no longer in service, the original behemoth of a coal-burning furnace still sits in the basement, a silent testimony to the sheer BTUs it took to heat this house before insulation, new windows, and more efficient zoned propane boilers came along.

My great-great-grandfather farmed 2,000 acres here with his brother. He was a huge cattle guy. The railroad spur came up into our property, and he would send cattle to Chicago on that. The track was taken out in the late 1970s, but in dry years, you can still see it. Those 2,000 acres were then divided among their three children.

The 700 acres of farmland we now have were incorporated in the late 1970s and named Maple Edge Farm. My parents started transferring shares to my sister and me as soon as they could, maximizing the yearly gifts they could make. My grandfather almost lost the farm when his parents died and he had to pay inheritance taxes, and he spent years getting the farm back on track. That was a big lesson for my parents. He and my grandmother were savers—neither a borrower nor lender be. *Debt* was a bad four-letter word to them.

Growing up, I remember playing outside all day with my sister. We rode wagons, played hide-and-seek, and pretended to be the "Dukes of Hazzard." When I got older, I would go down to the river. I also remember waking up in the summer and hearing the mourning doves, wrens, and robins. I was so glad I didn't have to go to school!

The magnolia tree would bloom right before planting. When the cicadas came out, I knew summer was half over, and that made me have a pit in my stomach. I remember eating strawberries right out of the garden. I remember waking up and seeing the floodwaters from the Nishnabotna and worrying whether they would come up to the house.

I didn't know until I went to college that others didn't have the stable childhood I did. My parents and grandparents provided me with such an amazing life. There is such turmoil in the world; I wish others could have what I have. Our son needs to understand that he's very lucky, and he should be compassionate with others. I know that if I were in trouble, my family would always be there for me.

When I graduated from high school, Dad told me I had to go to college, so I went to Drake University. After I finished at Drake, I worked construction in Des Moines for a year. I didn't get pressure to come back, but I wanted to. Hay was my first job on the farm. My dad said,

"Good luck, this is yours." Then the cows became mine, and finally the corn and soybeans. But really my dad and I still make decisions together, and he still helps out with the corn and soybeans. We had wheat at one point, and now I am interested in bringing it back. There is less pasture on this farm than in the past.

The technology changes, even since I started farming, have been amazing: GPS, yield monitors, computers in your pocket with our phones. You can collect data so much easier, and then make decisions based on it. I take pictures of what's going on in my fields and send them to my agronomist. And the creature comforts in the tractor, like heat and air-conditioning!

How crazy $400 an acre rent is! We have so many government programs that help us, but they also make you complacent. We don't try to innovate. Having a little pain isn't such a bad thing.

I want to keep harmony among family members, among neighbors, and with those who aren't part of this farming community. This is a place of solace, and our friends enjoy coming out here to visit from Omaha and other places. I want the farm to bring our family together, not drive us apart.

I would like to keep the farmland together, but it could be there is a compelling reason to split it up in the future. I also want to provide a place for someone to have a decent job here. I don't want to work twelve hours a day, seven days a week, and I am thinking about that now that my dad is retiring. I may hire someone full time. It is hard, though, to think about having someone here full time who is not family!

I am very attached to the land. I want to ensure my son is taken care of and the land stays in the family. So we've been proactive from the beginning on that. If Anderson wants to farm, I'd like to provide land for him, but I do not want to force it on him.

My top goal for my farmland is to use it to conserve or improve soil, increase biodiversity, improve water quality and other conservation. If we start regenerating soils, a lot of other environmental issues will be easier to solve. It is important to decide where we want this farm to go, so our family is working on a holistic farm goal. I want to get off of the 300-bushel-yield mindset and into regenerating the land. Iowa loses an average of five tons of topsoil per acre. We don't even have the basic tenets of good stewardship down!

I also want to use my farmland to benefit a worthy cause that is part of a larger whole. The family farm can be isolating. At the same time, what we do affects all those around us. If we can share our stories, we can all become better stewards of the land without going broke. My neighboring farmer friend Steve McGrew, for example, has been such an inspiration. I hope his farm and ours will be seen as centers of sustainable agriculture. As PFI cofounder Dick Thompson said, why would someone want to beat their neighbor by a bushel? My goodness. Neighbors should be sharing.

Constant Miracles from Tiny Seeds
by Angela Tedesco, Johnston, Iowa

Turtle Farm, a 20-acre farm located at Granger, Iowa, is a diverse organic vegetable farm for Community Supported Agriculture (CSA).[1] I have grown more than thirty types of vegetables and fruit and hundreds of varieties on this farm.

My husband, John, and I have owned the farm since 1998. Because we were already settled in our home in Johnston when we purchased it, we do not live at the farm. After I graduated from Iowa State University with a degree in horticulture, I rented ground for three years while we searched for ground to purchase. We had been searching for land closer than the rented grounds I had been using the previous three years, which were all 30 minutes away from home.

Over the years, I grew the CSA from 30 to 180 members. The farm also became more mechanized, although not as much as it could have been if I had been a more skilled farmer and purchased more equipment sooner. In the beginning years, I hired people to till the garden in the spring and to spread compost at times, and I purchased straw from others for use on the farm. Since no one lives at the farm, I have chosen not to have animals. Animals would have made it a more holistic farm.

In the beginning, I set up a hoop house and moved in a walk-in cooler that were purchased from other farms. The hoop house was used originally for in-ground production of a few crops, but later just for transplant production. A canopy was set up initially by the cooler to work under, but eventually I had a barn built and used one side of it for packing produce and a farm stand area, and the other for equipment storage. I had a deep well drilled when the farm was purchased, since vegetables and fruit are difficult to grow reliably without irrigation. Since the land was bare ground (we purchased 20 acres off of a 99-acre farm), we also installed a driveway.

The farm had been previously farmed conventionally, so it was three years before it could be certified organic. Since I was no longer on rented ground, I planted perennial crops—asparagus and berries—that my customers had been requesting. I also planted blueberries, but quickly learned how attractive they were to deer and decided I would not plant them again until I was willing to fence them.

At one point, I received a Trees Forever grant to plant crops in the buffer zone of the farm. A buffer zone is required around organic crops to protect them from potential chemical drift from neighboring farms and homes. I planted peach trees, hazelnuts, elderberries, and red twig dogwood alongside a row of evergreens. Unfortunately (or fortunately, for space for tractor turnaround and mowing), the evergreens did not survive.

Beehives serviced by others have come and gone at the farm. I added heat to the hoop house when I started transplant sales. I used a heated glass greenhouse at my home in Johnston to start transplants in the winter, reducing the need to drive to the farm.

As I gained farming experience, I added U-pick strawberries. U-pick customers were asking what else was available for purchase on the farm, so eventually I added a farm stand and sold excess produce on Wednesday evenings and Saturday mornings.

When Ben Saunders, who had been a part-time employee for several years, was added as a full-time employee and then farm manager, I tried to ease out of farming. We added two other enterprises to support this transition: organic transplant sales to the public and other organic growers in the spring, and extending the CSA season with a fall share in the month of October. After phasing out over two years, I retired from active farming at the end of 2012. The farm is now rented to Ben, who continues to produce organic transplants and a CSA (Wabi Sabi Farm).

I remember so many things about the farm: Dewdrops on leaf margins and spiderwebs. Birds of all kinds—from bluebirds and barn swallows to white pelicans and raptors—overhead. Emerging plants that line up and down the row and transition to lush full-grown plants loaded with fruit. A room or cooler full of harvested veggies and fruits, and the packed boxes for customers.

I remember the sounds of the meadowlarks and killdeer in the spring and the hawks screeching overhead, raindrops on the hoop-house plastic, and the clicking of the stirrup or wheel hoe as it moves through the soil. And of course, mosquitoes buzzing.

I love the aroma of basil if brushed and other herbs from rosemary to lavender, a barn full of freshly harvested garlic and ripe straw-berries in the heat of the day. The scent of tomato foliage as I trellised or picked them was pungent, and the scent of blooming thistle (ouch!) was sweet.

I remember the feel of firm, squeaky cabbage, pulling potatoes out of the soil, the itchy yet soft pubescence of okra, and the itchy spines of cucumbers and squashes. I loved tasting the first crops in the field as they ripen, especially asparagus, radishes, sugar snap peas, straw-berries, raspberries, and cherry tomatoes.

Each year the weather is a different challenge, which makes it hard to get good at doing this thing called farming. The animals and insects on the farm were continuous companions, teachers, inspiration, and indicators of health. The crops were returning friends each year who provided me with constant miracles of the bounty of food from tiny seeds. Where else could I find Hakurei turnips, Amish Paste or Gar-den Peach tomatoes, Rosa Bianca eggplant, and Amish Pie pumpkin?

It is an intense experience to dive in, plan, and execute produc-ing food for so many people each year. It is like birthing a child, with a similar load of responsibility, given the commitment. I found such joy in educating people about the farm, their food, and the process of getting food to their table. The whole experience gave me such a gift of spirituality.

I appreciate the people who accompanied me on this journey, espe-cially those employees, customers, and volunteers who returned for more than one season and understood that this is such a special en-deavor where much is required of you, but much is given in return. My associations with colleagues that began in the Iowa Network for Community Agriculture and continued with Practical Farmers of Iowa were so necessary and fulfilling for the success of the farm.

The number one goal for my farmland is to keep it as a farm for someone to continue using it in a sustainable manner, preferably organic. The farm is on the edge of the town of Granger, and selling it to anyone without this goal would very likely mean it would become a housing development. The farm went from being a conventional one to an organic one that is a diverse reservoir of wildlife, insects, and soil life that took years to develop. How the land is used could certainly vary from the use of the farm by one family, to joint ownership by several or numerous families, to use as an educational "opportunity" by a nonprofit. Depending upon its use, it could also serve as a model of urban agriculture, showing ways that land can be preserved even with development.

With this farm, I was able to figure out "what I wanted to do when I grew up," even if I was in my forties, and to go on and be able to accomplish it with some success. The farm was and still is a good educational tool. In its now urban environment, it stands as a beacon for preserving land for farming over development.

The Right Family at the Right Price
by Teresa Opheim

If it takes a village to raise a child, as an old adage says, how can the children, having left the village, repay and help sustain it? The village in this instance had provided an extra measure of support to a mother and her three young children when death took the father.

Former Montgomery County, Iowa, farmland owners Dale Nimrod and his siblings, Faith Sherman and Vance Nimrod, came up with a response that enabled a family active in their home community to take over their farm. The family, unknown to the owners, was selected because of their participation in community and church and their demonstrated desire to own and operate a farm there. A creative approach to pricing the transfer was obviously necessary.

But let's start at the beginning.

Leonard Nimrod, the father in this story, grew up on a farm near Stanton settled by his Swedish immigrant parents, stayed on, and shared in its operation. In 1934, he married a schoolteacher, Janet Meyers, recently transplanted from New York. By 1944, Janet and Leonard had managed to cobble together financing needed to purchase a farm of their own a couple miles away. They looked forward to the March 1 possession date, when they would move their three young children to the farm.

But in February, Leonard was diagnosed with a brain tumor. While doctors were trying to save him with surgery, Janet arranged the farm move from his hospital room in Omaha. Leonard died that July and never got to farm the new place. At the time, Dale Nimrod was five; his brother, Vance, was eight; and his sister, Faith, was just two. Janet decided to stay on the farm.

"My mother looked on staying as a kind of calling that we should be raised at that place," Dale says. "She managed to make it work. The church and the community were very instrumental in making it possible. I'm sure they put in the first crop. Countless acts of kindness followed. When the dad of a friend of mine, for example, was going to buy cattle in Omaha, he thought I should be along to learn how to do that. It was just acts like that, on and on and on, a support network that was very tangible."

The three kids thrived in this supportive community and then left for college and careers. Dale married Sunny, and they raised their three sons in the rolling hills near Decorah, where Dale taught chemistry at Luther College. Vance settled in Mississippi and Faith in Des Moines.

Janet continued to live on the farm and eventually transferred ownership to her three children, each getting 80 acres. The cropland was jointly rented out. In 2004, the farm manager—who in 1948, unmarried and twenty-four years old, had moved out to the Nimrod Farm to work the place—decided to retire from farming. "By that time it was clear that none of us siblings, now in our sixties, was interested in taking up farming or moving back to our hometown. So it was time to turn the farm over to someone else."

Dale says: "We were no different from many aging landowners facing this very common situation—we aspired to find a nice young family who would appreciate the land, the community, and the church, and would invest themselves in caring for all three. But far too often I have seen owners who fervently hope for such an outcome put their place up for auction with little more than their fingers crossed regarding their community. It is a misperception, I think, that selling to the highest bidder is the only way to be fair when disposing of property. We were determined to make the desired outcome a reality, and we were convinced that such an outcome would go much farther than, say, making a cash gift in sustaining community."

There are other ways of benefiting community through donations directly to, for example, a local church, but Dale reports, "I did not want to transfer our farm that way. Oftentimes with land donations when that strategy is used, the land is viewed as a financial investment and not, for example, as a strategy to keep farmers on the land or benefit conservation. If someone offers to donate a farm to a college, the college usually makes it very clear that it is not in the business of managing farms and that it will sell the farm upon receiving title to it, usually to the highest bidder. I think (and hope) most charitable institutions are up-front with potential donors in this regard."

Dale started by calling the Lutheran pastor in Stanton and asked for names of anybody who might be looking to farm. "That's how we connected with Mark Peterson," Dale recalls. "He had established himself and shown interest in the town and interest in the church. Mark was renting some land and owned some machinery, and this was really the kind of thing he was looking for. So we worked through how to establish a purchase price." The Nimrods asked the Petersons to use some farm productivity spreadsheets from Iowa State University to calculate the production value of the farmland, which, as Dale says, "has little, if anything, to do with the market price." Mark put together a cash flow statement, which included a land payment to the Nimrods. He based it on 2004 prices and yields, and a land payment based on the interest rate at the time and twenty years worth of payments.

"We wanted to get close to the real economic value of the farm, which is below the market price, of course," Dale reports. "We siblings looked over the figures carefully and concluded he did his calculations correctly. Then we set the purchase price at 25 percent higher than its calculated production value."

Mark Peterson says, "When Dale first called, I thought he was looking for an agent to sell the farm, and I had my real estate license. Then the lightbulb went on. Dale said he wanted to sell the farm to us. I said that we weren't in the position to buy a farm. He said, stick with me and we'll figure it out. Dale and his family had deep ties to the farm, but they could see that there was no one in their family who could carry it on, and they wanted it to be a family farm. He wanted to give someone the chance to make it on their own. In his own way, he was trying to keep Stanton going."

Mark and his wife, Melanie, also made two major investments to achieve the happy ending of this story. The second was a number of major land improvements, including his recent work with Practical Farmers to add cover crops. The first was to use their home equity in Stanton to buy back the acreage that contained the farmhouse, which the Nimrods had earlier sold off. The Petersons evicted the raccoons, renovated the house, and moved their family of five boys from town to the country to their new home on their new farm.

Reports Dale Nimrod: "We are just enormously pleased that this farm is in the Petersons' hands. I hear about people who have land for sale, and it's like it would be a sin if you sold it for less than what an auctioneer could get for you. I just can't understand it. There are things more important and much more satisfying than money."

A More Complete Farm

by Vic and Cindy Madsen, Audubon, Iowa

9

Cindy, Eric, and Vic Madsen.

VIC MADSEN

I recently sat down and thought about the past, present, and future of Madsen Stock Farm. What is meaningful about the farm? What memories do I want future generations to know about? And what are my overall goals for the farm thirty years from now?

Cindy and I purchased our home property in 1975 and moved here and raised our three sons. About ten years ago, we purchased another 80 acres that are nearby; together those 225 acres are owned free and clear. We also rent 90 acres nearby. There have been two owners on the rented ground—an estate and an off-farm investor. He bought it in 1988, and his daughter now manages it.

We bought the property because it had cattle feeding facilities. And we fed cattle until 1984, when the government began the dairy cow buyout program, which totally pulled the rug out from under the beef cattle market. When our feeders went to market ten months later, they weren't worth much because of the huge supply of meat on the market.

We've raised hogs here pretty much all the time. I was part of a farrowing co-op until 1999. Then I sold my shares because I didn't feel comfortable with gestation stalls and the other ways we were raising hogs. We then started farrowing on our own. We added beef cows seven to eight years ago. We really enjoy the beef cows. Cindy also raises a couple thousand broilers a year, which she direct markets.

We were traditional corn-bean conventional farmers until 2000. Ron Rosmann [an organic PFI farmer] tried for ten years to get me to go organic. He finally succeeded in 1998, when we started transitioning some ground. Now we have a variety of rotations: Corn/beans/oats/hay. Corn/beans/wheat. Corn/oats/hay. We run a different rotation on every field, depending on the hill slope.

We added about 300 aronia bushes in 2008. They are kind of fun. I'd never had any fruit crops before. It's not a big income thing, but it has helped us diversify, and it makes the farm a more pleasant place to live.

Cindy does the poultry work. She's on hand to chase hogs and calves or cows. Until our youngest son, Eric, got older, she hauled all the grain from the combine into town. She put a lot of hours on the 4440 tractor hauling grain in the fall. Eric got started farming when he was a freshman in high school, about ten years ago. He has a knack with the mechanical part, which I'm not good at. He does the machinery management. I have done the livestock thing. Today we all do what has to be done. I still like to plant; he runs the combine.

Our oldest son, Jeff, works for a seed corn company. We were Pioneer dealers, maybe that's why he got into that. Our middle son, Mark, earned a Ph.D. in biochemistry and genetics and moved to California. He and his wife are pretty well established there.

The older two boys grew up when we were having a difficult time farming. They saw that, and it probably soured them on farming. Farming then, in the 1980s, totally changed my farm management philosophy. It is so important to have animals on the farm and to have diverse enterprises so you don't have all of your eggs in one basket.

Cindy Madsen, with daughter-in-law Ashley and son Eric.

The current crash in grain prices [2014–2015] and the boom in the cattle business are good examples.

We really enjoy growing organically. I don't think I'd be farming today if it wasn't for the organic, both financially and personally. Organics is much more of a challenge. Conventional farming wasn't very fun anymore, because you had to deal with chemical salesmen, and they'd always be changing the prices and changing the names on chemicals. With conventional farming, there were more unpleasant jobs, like getting fertilizer put on. With organic, I feel like I'm a lot more in control, and we don't have to deal with all the chemicals.

When the boys were little, we used chemicals. When Jeff and Mark were about eight and ten, we had seeded some oats. We were out there digging in the ground to see how deep the seeds were. And that was fun. The boys wanted to do it with the corn too, but I couldn't let them because of the insecticide on the corn. I can still see how sad they were that they couldn't dig for the seed. With organic, kids can dig for the seed.

Many say the neatest thing about fall is driving a combine and listening to an Iowa State football game, and I kind of agree with that.

I really like the smell of harvested corn. Since I've become organic, I notice the spring smells a lot more. Our soil when we were conventional was pretty much odorless. Now when we till in the spring, we get that earthy smell I remember as a kid growing up. Cindy Cambardella [a soil scientist] says that it is probably actinomycetes that give off that odor, and they are associated with healthy soil. I feel like we're doing the right thing when I smell that.

I also like the smell of alfalfa hay after it's cut. I like walking in the hog barn and hearing the sows grunting while they are nursing their pigs. I know everyone is healthy and well when I hear that. I like the sight of the corn peeking through the soil. Usually the first week, ten days after planting, I go out every day and check each field on the four-wheeler, if I have time, because that new plant coming through the ground is such a miracle. Plus I check for errors in planting.

June is probably Iowa's prettiest time. You can still see between the rows of the corn. The beans are up and need to be cultivated. Oats don't have weeds yet. The hay is green and lush. The whole farm scene in June is beautiful.

My low moments on the farm are dragging out a dead pig or calf. Anytime I lose an animal it bothers me. My peak moments include seeing a load of finished hogs go up the chute, because, when you farrow to finish, those hogs represent an awful lot of work.

One of my favorite memories on the farm is when the two oldest boys were about nine and seven, and they came around the corncrib carrying a bag of popcorn they had picked all by themselves. They were grinning from ear to ear. Cindy and I didn't know they were picking the popcorn. They could barely lift the bag, which was the first bag of the year, and they had carried it quite a ways. Both had looks of joy, pride, and a sense of accomplishment.

Now that we are organic, I kind of like filling a semi with grain because I realize that it's a lot more work. We tilled the ground, kept the weeds under control, and did all the machinery part.

In thirty years, my goals for the farm include improving soil conservation, biodiversity, and water and air quality on the farm. To have helped make my heirs more financially stable through the sale of or rental income from the farm. And to keep the farmland together as a working farm. These goals are medium priorities.

My top farm goal for the future is to keep family harmony, to keep my family from fighting about what happens to or on the farm. My second goal is to provide a home for a family to live on the farm and work the ground. A farm is a wonderful place for children. Looking at the farm in thirty years, I'd like to see little kids running around. A farm is more complete when there are little kids on it. I enjoy that so much.

CINDY MADSEN

I was born and raised on a farm, and I can't see myself doing anything else. I love the smell of fresh mowed hay and the apple tree blooming just south of the driveway. I love the smell of fresh wood chips under the baby chicks when we first take them out of the box. I love baby kittens and newborn calves; they are so soft. The rolling hills on our farm are beautiful. I like to see the different colors through the seasons, even winter. Some of the trees are just gorgeous with the ice and frost on them.

I have many memories of the fun I had taking the boys to 4-H and Boy Scout events, but there were also many challenges to raising three boys on a farm. Three events stand out in our family history; they get retold many times. When Eric was born, Mark was seven years old and Jeff was nine. I remember when Eric was just a month or so old, I went to his bassinet and to my surprise I found a very real looking big black spider on Eric's forehead—Jeff and Mark had put the plastic spider there and were waiting to see my reaction. When Eric was about four, Mark came carrying a bleeding little Eric in his arms up to the house, Eric repeating, "Don't tell Mom, don't tell Mom." Long story short: Eric riding a four-wheeler (not allowed), loose gravel, wooden post, lots of blood, hospital emergency room, seven stitches to Eric's head.

Another time I happened to look out the kitchen window to see Jeff and Mark on the four-wheeler doing little circles with Eric on a plastic sled tied about 15 feet out going in very fast circles. The sled hits a little gravel, stops, and Eric went scooting off the sled on his tummy for about 20 feet. Luckily, he was bundled up pretty good and he didn't hit anything. I wonder how many other things happened that I never heard about or didn't catch as I looked out the window.

When we first married, we farrow-to-finished hogs, and then we became part of a feeder pig co-op. It was a milestone on our farm when we left the co-op. The hog confinement building had such an odor compared to the way we raise hogs now. The automatic feed system in the building always needed tending to. Sorting hogs from the confinement was difficult, because they were not used to the light or fresh air as they went up the chute and into the livestock trailer. Plus we wanted to keep control over what the animals got fed, and we couldn't do that with the co-op. We like to raise our animals naturally without any added antibiotics or hormones.

I like to do anything on the farm that involves the outdoors. I like to take care of my chickens. I especially like caring for cattle. I love my direct marketing, which I've done since 1987. I started out with a few chickens, and it just snowballed. In direct marketing, I meet so many interesting people and have made lifelong friends. I have learned so much from them.

Vic takes care of production on the farm, and corn and bean sales. I take care of the bookkeeping and the direct market sales. If someone has questions about feed, I refer them to Vic. I do the insurance; he does all the government program stuff. I'm a morning person and he's a night person, and that's probably why we get along.

When the boys were young, I helped in the field a lot. Vic was on the combine, and I hauled in. Now when Vic and Eric are busy in the field, I help out with the hog and cattle chores. Pulling out someone who is stuck in the mud or snow is my least favorite task on the farm. Vic and Eric aren't in the best mood to start with when they get stuck, and then they have to come and get me to help them. I either go too fast or too slow. I don't get the hand signals right. I'm never doing the right thing.

We have an organic operation because we like to build soil health. We also think it is important to have livestock on the farm. If you have livestock, you have the manure to provide a natural fertilizer for the soil. The small grains and clover prepare the field for the corn; the beans following corn put nitrogen in the soil to feed the small grains. We feed the corn to the livestock. The livestock manure then feeds the crop ground again. It's a more sustainable circle.

When you have grains and livestock, you are busy year-round. Plus, with so many enterprises, we balance the debt flow during the year. If you have a failure in one area, hopefully the other enterprises will make up for that failure. Last summer we lost two of our hoop houses in that July windstorm. We had to sell the sows and the boar because we didn't have room for them. So from March until October, we did not have whole or half hogs for sale. We filled in with chickens and other enterprises.

Many people say "get bigger," but when you get bigger, you need employees. Then you can have problems, like finding good, dependable help and then getting them to show up. Plus, are you actually making more money or are you just turning over more dollars?

I don't know what we would have done if Eric hadn't kept the farm running when Vic got colon cancer in 2010 and had open-heart surgery and a reaction to medicine in 2011. Eric is our mechanic, our plumber, our electrician. Jeff and Mark realize that Eric is around to help us. In our estate planning, we've tried to be fair. We have things worked out so that if something happens to us, Eric gets first opportunity to farm the ground. We do charge him the same amount of rent we pay our landlord, because we don't think it's fair to the other boys if we didn't.

A while back, the group of us in Audubon County Family Farms hired a tour bus from the Des Moines Farmers Market. A grandfather and his two-year-old grandson were on the bus. At our place, the grandfather took a picture of this little boy in the bean field. The grandfather talked a lot about that trip to our farm. About a year later, the little boy's mother came to my booth at the farmers market and told me that the grandfather had passed away. In his casket, they included the picture of the little boy in the bean field because visiting our farm meant so much to the grandfather. It brought tears to my eyes.

The first year we sold quarters, halves, and wholes of beef, a young gentleman placed an order. He said his dad used to raise cattle, and he'd like to come to the farm sometime. I asked him if he wanted to bring his dad along and pick out his own beef. One nice day here came that guy and his dad from Des Moines. Our cattle are fairly tame, so we walked down into the lot. Vic told him which ones would be going to slaughter, and he took his pick. The young man told me that meant so much to his dad. We have a lot of stories like that.

I hope Vic's and my health stay such that we can keep our livestock operation and help out later on. We both enjoy the farm so much.

Thirty years from now, I want people to remember that the farm was organic and sustainable. We tried to improve the soil to pass on to future generations. I also want people to know that the farm was profitable. And that we got along well in managing and working the farm.

My goals for the farmland are to provide a farm for a family to work. And to give all of my heirs an inheritance valued the same. However, my top goal for our farmland is to keep it together and farmed sustainably. I would like the farm to stay together as a unit and in the family's name as long as possible. I would like to see a family member work the farm in the future, but if that doesn't work out, I'd rather not have it sold. Historically, farmland has been a good investment. Our farmland could be a source of income from cash rent for our heirs.

To Keep Family Harmony
by Barb Opheim, Mason City, Iowa

My family was the first to break the prairie on the 80 acres I now own. My grandfather Isaiah Fisher came to Pocahontas County in 1886 from Jasper County and bought the quarter section at $10 per acre. Shortly after, my dad recalled, Isaiah bought another 120 acres for $12.50 an acre. The land is fairly close to the Des Moines River, where people first settled because of the wood and water, but there were neither on what is now my 80 acres.

My grandparents married in 1886 and had a granary built on the land. They lived in the second story of the granary until the house was built. The first year he was here, Isaiah plowed 90 acres with a walking plow. My dad told me that a lot of the time his father went barefoot because the soil felt so good under his feet.

My dad was born on the farm in 1904; I was born on that same farm in 1935. We raised oats, soybeans, corn, and hay on the farm. The crops were rotated so that the same nutrients weren't taken out of the soil year after year. My dad used animal manure as fertilizer. We had chickens, hogs, sheep, and beef cows (rarely bulls—the artificial inseminator came for breeding). We had a small herd of dairy cows too. The pigs were attracted to people, but I sure wasn't attracted to them.

The animal babies were such a highlight. We always fed calves and lambs with a bottle. Once you started feeding them with a bottle, you were their best friend. One lamb followed me into the house one time. Baby chicks were marvelous, constantly making peep noises. Then when they were grown, the roosters would attack me. I would always tell the ones that took after me: "I took care of you when you were a baby. Why are you turning on me?"

We always had dogs, and there were lots of cats around the farm. We would try and find the new batches of kittens. I remember Mother telling me about a mother cat purring in the face at her daughter who was giving birth, then checking at the other end to see if the kittens were coming out. She was being a midwife!

We had two gardens, one for food and one for flowers. We had potatoes, beans, peas, carrots, tomatoes, all kinds of vegetables. We didn't buy much food; we canned our vegetables. I remember digging up potatoes in the fall, separating big ones from little ones, and then cooking the little ones first and storing the big ones in the basement.

The flower garden was south of the house. There was a big square "outdoor living room" where we cooked and entertained company in the summer. There were plants all around it: lilacs, corn lilies, hollyhocks, and peonies. I loved the smell of the lilacs.

The hay up in the haymow also had a good smell. We had a basketball hoop up there, and I played basketball. I also bounced a ball outside against the barn a lot.

I remember walking out in the fields when the crops were growing and the wind was blowing a little, and it would be very peaceful. Lying out in the hammock was so peaceful too. I spent a lot of time in that hammock. Rarely did a car go by; when one did, you knew who it was. There was a wooded area north of the house where we walked that was also very quiet.

I spent a lot of time alone. I didn't dislike living on the farm, but I would never have wanted to be a farmwife. It was a lonely place. You didn't see anybody. But the other side of it was you could also go anywhere around the farm with anything on, and you never had to close the shades.

The farm expanded through the years. At one point my mother and father each owned 200 acres. (My mother purchased farmland with the inheritance she received from her father, who was a doctor near Bloomfield.) My parents' will specified that the 40 acres of the homeplace be sold to cover estate taxes. Now there are corn and beans where the house, the farm buildings, the rest of the trees, and the gardens once were.

I'd prefer to keep my 80 acres in the family, but if my children aren't interested in keeping it or it is a hassle, I don't have a problem with selling it. It's like inheriting a house. If it doesn't work anymore for my children to own it, then that's the way it is. My children will have complete discretion over the farmland when I am gone.

I would like to keep the 80 acres together, rather than sold into smaller portions. I would like the land to provide a home for a family trying to make a living on the farm. I also would like the farm used to increase soil conservation and water quality.

However, my top goal for my farmland is to keep family harmony. I do not want my heirs to fight because of this land. I don't want anyone to feel like they didn't get a fair share. Wayne [her husband] and I are like that with everything.

Soils as God Intended

by Del Ficke, Pleasant Dale, Nebraska

11

To my future generations,

In 1860, Johann Ficke made the trip from Germany to settle in the United States. Just nine years later, after first arriving in Wisconsin, he found a beautiful spot a mile west of Pleasant Dale, Nebraska, to homestead and begin the labors that have become our family's legacy. In 1888, Johann purchased the farm I grew up on for my great-grandfather H. F. and his wife, Annette, when they got married. H. F. and Annette had four sons and two daughters—Frank, Fred, Hank, Mary, Helen, and my grandpa Adolph. Adolph and Lana had three children—Clifford, who tragically died at the age of three; my father, Kenneth; and a daughter, Ellen.

To this day, we are farmers and cattlemen—that is the core of our family's agricultural history. However, at the center of the story is family—we all live very close to one another. My sisters, Janet,

Rhonda, and Jolene, live within a section of my wife, Brenda; our daughter, Emily; and me. My mother, Beverly, lives just across the lawn from our house. I am also so proud to say that my son, Austin, and his wife, Alyssa, and baby daughter, Attley, are living in a cottage that we built for them directly west of our house as well. Needless to say, my heart bursts with the blessing of the seventh generation of Fickes living here today.

However, while genealogies are important, I write this letter to those who will come far after I am gone in order that you better understand the realities of carrying on a true family farming operation. The key is the family. This personal family story truly begins with my father, who was always putting himself aside so we would have a better life. His secret was simple—a lifelong commitment to clearly communicating to all of us how we were the most essential part of keeping the farm going. We were his legacy, not the land and the livestock, but rather the family he loved so much.

In the early '80s, Dad and Mom told my sisters and me to come around the table. They had a plan, and we were part of it. The plan was fair and equitable in that it was based on each of our levels of involvement in the farming operation. There were no issues, because we were all there to ask questions, and we respected what they were saying because it was coming from their mouths, not a piece of paper after they were gone. Their hearts and minds were in front of us, sharing their dreams and desires. As siblings, there is no going back on that because we all love each other, respect one another, and trust their plans.

Dad and Mom deeded the land to all of us kids and retained a life use of it (a life estate). They agreed to pay all expenses and get all the income from the land. My father has since passed away, so right now my mom rents all the land to me, and she pays taxes and also gets the cash rent income. In essence, I am paying for land that is already deeded to me. But that's okay because the land has always been protected and because as a family we have talked this through and clearly understand the intended purposes of this type of arrangement.

Growing up, my father sent me all over the country to learn about cattle and agriculture. When I was twenty years old, at Thanksgiving my dad announced to everyone, "Del will be in charge of the farming operation starting tomorrow morning." He hadn't told me that prior to that public announcement. But I understand why now. My dad wanted his son to understand how every part of the operation worked at a young age. He would often bring up stories of our neighbors with sons who were fifty to eighty years old and had no clue when the father passed away how to run the farm.

My father's decision to hand over the reins came with a lot of stress at times. However, the key factor was that he was alive to provide the guidance and allowed me to make the decisions. He ultimately watched me make a lot of mistakes and also achieve some successes. He did not cosign any notes. It was my business to run, profits and losses.

I built our farming operation to 7,000 acres of farmland and pastures for Ficke Cattle Company. I did this through relationship building and learning to adopt new practices to create more efficiencies. In 1987, I started no-tilling. For one growing season my dad would not talk to me about the crops because he was so dismayed about planting into the weeds and stalks. It turned out that first year of no-tilling was a very dry year. On Dad's tilled acres the yields suffered. However, on my end, the no-till acres had doubled in production over his tilled acres. Needless to say, Dad was a no-till fan after that.

In 1999, things dramatically changed again and needed to. I believe that when my back blew out that year, God was sending me a message about the future and what really matters about family farming. The farm boy was forced to rethink his life. I went to college because I couldn't physically farm that many acres and stay alive. During college, I was still managing all 7,000 acres. Then I decided to offer the farming opportunity to my nephews Matt and Ryan. In turn, I took a position managing a medical clinic in Lincoln, Nebraska, while still maintaining my cow herd.

Agriculture was always in my heart, though, and I have been blessed to see agriculture from so many points of view. Because of my experiences both on and off the farm, I have been inspired to embark on a new journey. Today, I am back home running this 500-acre farm. My goal is to restore and improve the soils back to the way God intended. A couple years ago we started implementing cover crops on our operation. We are also taking row-crop acres and putting them into season-long cover crop grazing scenarios and ensuring our native pastures are performing at their maximum potential.

We have trademarked our composite breed of cattle, Graze Master Genetics, which are suited for 100 percent forage-based programs. I am also doing consulting across the country on cattle and transitioning farms and ranches in a more holistic manner. My passion is taking what I have learned and helping others learn from my mistakes and successes along the way.

Most important, I feel like we are doing the right things again. We are enjoying the smell of sweet clover and alfalfa. We have a Russian immigrant and his son providing bees and producing honey that in turn give us healthier crops and pastures. There are a host of rewarding transformations taking place.

The farm is full of more birds than ever. I carry around a bird book so I can identify them. I also carry a range book and a cover crop book so I can identify the new plants coming up through the soil. We are also not irrigated, so water conservation issues are real and top of mind every day.

Improving the environment on this farm is a top goal. We have decreased the use of chemicals and synthetic fertilizers by 95 percent on our pastures. It's always about building up the soil and retaining the water. We also want to continue to make our farm a place where all our neighbors, both rural and urban, are welcome and can learn.

My grandpa Adolph's and my father's voices are my constant companions. Both of them were big on community and neighbors. Grandpa Adolph said, "The day the horses left and the tractor came was the day we replaced community with competition." He would constantly talk with me about the way we were doing things on the farm, and he didn't think things were going the right way. He was anti–too much government and anti–the overreach of corporations into farming and livestock. Grandpa Adolph certainly helped me be more discerning about what is being sold to the typical farmer—everything from equipment to chemicals. There's a lot of propaganda about what we really need and a lot more wisdom needed to actually make good decisions.

Like the generations before me, the family is the most important part of the farm. It is their talents and gifts that are the most precious resources. The land must be worked for and is not guaranteed, but the creativity of the next generation can keep the farm and Ficke Cattle Company going with new ideas and dreams.

Thirty years from now I want to be remembered for doing things the way God intended. Work has to mean something through the generations. There must be integrity—with your community, family, and the environment.

So be a Ficke! Do it your way, think on your own, and be independent.

Adams County Needs Young Farmers
by Neil Hamilton, Waukee, Iowa

My ancestors acquired my family's homeplace in Adams County, Iowa, in 1872 after they came out from Ohio. My great-grandfather prospered on that farm. It became a show farm, with one of the largest barns in that part of the state and a big house with a cement basement and running water. I bought that homeplace back in 1982 and later donated a portion that had never been plowed to the Adams County Conservation Board. It is now a restored prairie called Hamilton Prairie. I sold the farmhouse to a family who has worked to restore it.

My great-grandfather went on to acquire other farmland, which he gave to his children and the church when he died. Uncle Charlie got the homeplace, Aunt Jessie received another farm, and he gave the 200 acres I grew up on to my grandmother, Anna. My grandma was married to Mel Hamilton, a horse trainer and stockman. Dad remembers that Mel would leave on Monday and go farm to farm, trading animals. He apparently had a good eye for livestock. He would come back on Friday with cows and horses. He would feed out the cattle and train the horses. In 1916, my grandparents cashed out, moved to Southern California, and bought orange groves in what is now Irvine. With the decline in agriculture in the 1920s, things seemed to unravel for Mel and Anna and their six children.

In about 1933, Anna, my dad, and two of his brothers moved back to Iowa to live on the farm she had inherited. They were known locally as "the California Fools." Within a month, one brother headed back to California. Later, the other brother became a merchant marine.

So at twenty-two, my dad became a farmer. I can say—and if he were sitting here he wouldn't disagree—he was in some ways a prisoner to the farm. It wasn't what he would have chosen; it was chosen for him in many ways. But he did it for the rest of his life. He farmed until he was seventy-eight and lived until he was ninety-one.

My dad was bright, but he didn't expand the farm, and he didn't spend much time trying to be a better farmer. He enjoyed reading and traveling. We had the *Encyclopædia Britannica*, and we got the *Saturday Evening Review*. He was a great H. L. Mencken fan. In his youth he had worked at MGM Studios in California and had been a lifeguard at Balboa Beach, so he wasn't much like the farmers around him.

Dad married my mom in 1940. She was from a hardscrabble tenant farm family that moved year to year. When they met, she was a domestic in Creston, taking care of someone's kids. She was about five feet tall, weighed about ninety pounds, and was a beautiful girl.

During World War II, Dad got a farming deferment and was taking care of his mother. Being part of agriculture was a big part of the war effort, but it also meant he was out of danger. Later on, the veterans who came back to Adams County had a camaraderie that my dad wasn't a part of.

During the war, my folks moved to Southern California for a couple years, and Grandma Anna moved with them. I guess they thought there was a better life out there where he grew up. Dad managed a vegetable farm, and Mom worked in a munitions plant. But they came back to the farm. My brother was born in 1949, and I was born in 1954. My grandmother—who had lived with them for fifteen years by then—died a few years later.

At this point something that is fairly unusual, even today, kicked in: rather than leaving her land to my dad and his five siblings "to share and share alike," Anna left half of it to Dad and half of it in five pieces to the rest of them. In the will, there was a provision that Dad had the right to buy the pieces from them. That was an enlightened thing to do in the 1950s.

From my parents' perspective, they had earned it. They had taken care of Grandma and the farm. But the news didn't go down well with the other brothers and sisters. They were pressuring my dad to redivide the farm equally. For a period of time, there are some drafts of agreements between them, and my dad seemed to be giving in to his siblings, but then he decided not to do it. Later, he exercised his provision to buy the land and borrowed money from the Federal Land Bank. My folks spent the next fifteen to twenty years paying off these brothers and sisters for the other half of the farm so they could keep the farm intact. I remember the day when they finally paid off the loan.

Anna's will created a family schism, and that's why I didn't see those aunts and uncles for much of my childhood. Before then, some of the West Coast relatives had sent their kids back to the farm to live in the summertime. As a kid, I didn't know much about this family conflict.

When I was younger, we had corn, beans, hogs, cattle, chickens, and milking shorthorns on the farm. My mother had a big garden. We were relatively poor, but everyone around us was too. The farm always came first. There was running water to the tank before running water to the house. One of my early jobs was to carry buckets of water to the kitchen counter.

Even though we were poor, Christmas was a helluva big deal. My mom and dad remember me arguing with a neighbor about whether there was a Santa Claus. My argument was there had to be because there was no way my family could afford all the presents we got at Christmas. It turns out the Christmas money came from one of my dad's enterprises, custom baling. He had a WD45 Allis-Chalmers that had a round baler, and he'd go around and bale the neighbors' hay. So I later found out that we had received all this stuff because my parents had planned for it.

My mom and dad never wanted my brother and me to be farmers. I'm sure my dad said things like "If you ever want to be a farmer, I will kick you in the butt and send you back to college." Your parents always think you are brilliant. My dad's nickname for me was "professor." And now I have been one for thirty-five years! There was never a day I would miss school to work on the farm. A lot of kids would stay home and cultivate corn, but my dad would have thought that was crazy to cut into your education to farm. You didn't miss school to work.

So I went to Iowa State, then the University of Iowa law school. I wouldn't be in agricultural law if I hadn't come out of an agricultural background. And I wouldn't have been involved in all these farm policy issues either. If you are going to talk about food and farm policy and law, you should know why farmers do what they do.

By the 1970s, my dad was in his early seventies and still farming the 200 acres with his broken-down equipment. Neighbors were practically slobbering over themselves wanting to get his farm. By the Farm Crisis of the 1980s, many of those neighbors so keen to expand were out of business. Our land went down in value in the '80s, but we didn't owe anyone anything. So it was much more resilient in that regard.

We got rid of the cattle before I got out of high school. The pigs were gone even before I was in high school. The pastures were plowed up, fences taken out, and Dad planted the farm to all corn and soybeans. And it's been that way ever since. This was the period of Secretary of Agriculture Earl Butz and "get big or get out," the time of the massive Russian grain sale.

As soon as I left home, my folks started going away in the wintertime. Come the first week in November, they'd close the door, put a blanket over the TV, and go down to Texas outside of Corpus Christi. It was cheaper for them to rent a place in south Texas than to heat the drafty old farmhouse. They didn't have anything to do on the farm in the wintertime anyway. I honestly think getting away in the wintertime extended their lives twenty years. They had a lot of friends down there.

They went south until the year before my mom died at eighty-one. She fell down the stairs and broke her neck in the year 2000. Dad was in the nursing home with dementia and didn't know she was gone. The 200-acre farm had become 160 before he died because we had to sell off the back 40 to pay the nursing home bills. If he had lived long enough, we would have had to sell the whole damn place.

When my dad died, I got the north 80 and my brother got the south 80. My brother sold right away to Ray Gaesser, who was a mile down the road and had been farming it for years. When we had to sell the 40 acres for the nursing home bills, we had sold them to Ray as well.

I held on to my 80 for another ten years. I had told Ray that if I was ever going to sell it, I wasn't going to put it up for auction. He is a good farmer with a son, Chris, now farming with him. Hell, he already owned the back 40, my brother's 80, and another 20 acres adjacent to our farm. It was inevitable that I would sell to him.

We decided to sell when we did because the land had increased in value so much. And I thought, "Do I really need this land?" I don't have a little Jimmy coming along. I thought, "I can get x in cash rent but sell it for y and get annual rental payments through a land installment contract." I do have to pay capital gains taxes; the basis was stepped up at the time I inherited the land.[1]

If we want to have new farmers, we need landowners who are going to get out of the way and sell their land. Chris has a wonderful operation he's going to step into with Ray and his mom. He didn't have any land he owned himself, so I sold my 60 acres to him. We have a fifteen-year land contract with a balloon payment at the end. There is a provision in the contract that if, after a certain number of years of payment, he wants to build a house where my family's farmhouse used to be, we will survey off a 5-acre portion and give him title to it so he owns that free and clear. Under a land contract, you don't really own any of it until you pay off the entire land contract.

Could I have gotten more for my family farmland? Sure, I could have started a bidding war and made Chris pay more. I could have sold it to a wealthy individual as an investment. But money isn't everything. I have never regretted selling. I never think, "How could I sell my heritage?" If I felt the urge to see my heritage, I would go down to Hamilton Prairie [the land he donated to the Adams County Conservation Board in 2005]. It is one of my favorite places to walk.

At some point, I might run out of money and wish I had sold that farm for more. I hope that doesn't happen, but if it does, I won't have anyone to blame but myself. Adams County needs young farmers owning a piece of land more than it needs people who used to live there hanging on to farmland and pretending they're still farmers. As John Baker of the Beginning Farmer Center says: "You don't own a farm; you own a piece of farmland. It stopped being a farm when your family left it." A farm is a family, a piece of land, a business, an entity. People need to recognize that.

Historically, this nation's preference was not for tenancy but to convert tenants into owners. In the 1940s, tenancy was almost seen as an evil. There was the ladder you moved up from being a hired employee, to tenant, to being an owner. Ownership was the goal for a lot of reasons. For security. For wealth creation. For stewardship. Not many people would choose to always be a tenant if they could own the land.

Many people seem to feel different about tenancy today, as if ownership was not really an important issue. Now people say things like "Why would you tie all your money up in land? You should own machinery, let others own the land." But land tenure issues—who owns the land, how it is farmed and by whom, and who has access to it—are critical for agriculture but also for a healthy, sustainable food system.

Landownership provides the stability, the autonomy, the opportunity for long-term planning and investment, and the wealth creation potential that is central to our agricultural history. Farmers who own their land have more security and autonomy. They don't deal with landlords coming and saying, "Well, you've been renting this land for forty years, now I am going to put this on the market, so find something else to do." There's also the idea that "the footsteps of the owner are the best fertilizer": owners will make the investment in the land long-term, planning the future in conservation. "Farming a piece like it's rented ground" has some truth to it. That doesn't mean that owners can't abuse the land or have short-term economic challenges, but if people are there on short-term rent, there is no reason you would assume they are going to take care of it like they own it. You don't go wash your rental car before you take it back.

How different would the state look if all the people who owned the land didn't farm it and all we had were tenants? Corn would still get planted, but it has a whole helluva different social and economic impact. When farmers who own their land are profitable, the money goes back into their own farms and into their communities.

Legally, can we stop nonfarmers from owning farmland? Well, no. Individuals can buy as much land as they want if they can afford it. But if farmers must be tenants, is that healthiest for the land, the future, and our communities?

Checklist for Resiliency
by Margaret McQuown and Steve Turman,
Red Oak, Iowa

MARGARET MCQUOWN

My husband and I are proud to be making our retirement home the farm that has been in my family for over 115 years. In 1899, my great-grandparents—John Erwin and Retta Eliza Taylor—named it Pleasant Prospects Farm. In 2012, my husband and I renamed it Resilient Farms, which we feel better reflects the current situation and the challenges we face in managing our farmland for the future.

My farm sits on a hillside 1.5 miles west of Red Oak, Iowa. It is 167 acres with 132 acres of no-till row crops (in a traditional corn-soybean rotation) and 35 acres of buildings, conservation reserve, and woodlands. Notable features of the farm include a 115-year-old five-bedroom Victorian farmhouse, a large bank barn, a 1920 clay-tile grain bin, a clay-tile silo, three metal Quonsets/sheds, several metal grain bins, a 3-acre black walnut plantation, and a creek bordered by old and new riparian buffers. As a pioneer of conservation, my great-grandfather added terraces and an evergreen windbreak in 1921.

My grandmother—Laura Taylor McQuown—moved with her parents to this farm as a small girl. She was an only child, so it's hard to imagine how she felt growing up in such a large house in the early 1900s.

My grandparents—Laura and Earl McQuown Sr.—moved with their three children—Ruth, Earl Jr., and Annabel—to this house when my dad was eight. He had great memories of growing up on the farm. When Dad returned from World War II, he bought the farm from Grandpa, started farming, and brought my mom—Gretchen McQuilkin Isebrands—to the farm when they married in 1947.

I was the youngest of four kids—two boys and two girls. A bit of a tomboy, I tried to keep up with my brothers so they would include me in their adventures. We loved to swing on the rope in the barn's hayloft, swim in the ponds, and play in the creek. I was the guinea pig for my brothers' big ideas. When I was five, they built a pulley swing from our tree house to another tree. They said, "Marg, why don't you go first?" I fell, sprained my ankle, and had to go to school wearing my bedroom slippers. How embarrassing! Another time they built a raft, stuck me on it, and pushed it to the center of the pond to see if it would float. They didn't think whether or not I could swim to shore if it sank! We climbed the pine trees west of the house and played Davy Crockett and Daniel Boone in the big evergreen windbreak, building forts with fallen limbs, "stalking" big game for dinner, or "fighting" vicious Indians. After big snowstorms, we dug snow caves in the giant drifts and sledded down the backyard hill across the east driveway and into the ditch along the highway.

4-H was an important part of my life. My mint jelly and apricot/pineapple jam entry won a purple ribbon at the county fair and a blue one at the state fair. I spent hours picking, cleaning, and straining the mint leaves for the jelly. It all paid off! My family wasn't so excited about the multiple test batches of scalloped eggplant I made for another 4-H project. After it was over, we never ate eggplant again!

Another 4-H adventure was riding my horse Thunder to town for the county fair. My final year in 4-H was the first year our fair had a horse show. I had dreamed of showing Thunder at the fair for years, so I was determined to get him there. We didn't have a horse trailer, and Thunder refused to go up the loading chute into the truck, so I had no choice but to ride him. Luckily, we only lived 1.5 miles from town.

Many times I rode Thunder Indian-style (no saddle or bridle, just holding on to his mane). I would jump on him in my swimsuit and tennis shoes and gallop across the pasture. Thunder and I would journey a mile west along the highway to my friend Carol's house. Since Carol also owned a horse, we loved riding together. She was my nearest nonsibling playmate and a fellow 4-Her.

I loved to ride the tractor and combine with my dad. I wanted to drive the tractor, but my dad had a very peculiar idea about this. Since I had two older brothers, Dad would say, "Only poor farmers make their daughters drive a tractor working the fields." I liked watching him repair his equipment. My sister and I detasseled seed corn for DeKalb. For two summers, I organized a crew of friends from town to weed soybeans. Detasseling and walking beans were the best-paying summer jobs available. And we had the craziest fun working under the blazing hot sun!

When I graduated Iowa State University in 1974, my present was a one-way ticket to New York City, where a fashion stylist position with Vogue/Butterick Pattern Company awaited me. I pursued a thirty-seven-year career in the fashion, marketing, advertising, and fundraising industries in New York, Chicago, and Dallas. Dad called me in New York once and said, "Why don't you come back and run the farm?" My reply: "I know nothing about agriculture." He said that I was a good businessperson and could learn the farming part. I didn't take his offer seriously, nor did I understand the importance of this vote of confidence on his part. Now I guess things have come full circle. Throughout my career I always lived in cities, but my love for the farm—our farm—has remained strong!

In 1976, Mom and Dad moved to a house in town while continuing to actively farm. In the mid-1980s, Dad farmed 1,350 acres, a combination of owned and rented land. In 1989, they sold the farm equipment and shifted to a 50/50 crop-share arrangement with a young farmer. Dad died in 1990. Mom continued to crop-share and enjoyed playing an active role in the farm management. Mom finally decided to cash rent in 2008 at the age of eighty-nine.

Mom died suddenly on December 29, 2008. My siblings and I were co-executors—an unusual arrangement. We all had to work together and mutually agree on the estate settlement, and it worked! We encountered a situation that challenges many estates of farm and small-business owners. In 2008, the estate tax exemption was $2 million; in 2009, it increased to $3.5 million. Mom's health had been so good that her estate plan was based on her reaching the $3.5 million exemption date. We were forced to sell 160 acres to pay the HUGE inheritance tax. If Mom had just lived two more days!

One brother didn't want farmland while three of us did, so we gave his share of the estate in cash. The three of us own separate pieces of farmland, but from an operational standpoint, we run the 508 acres as one farm. We rent the land to our farmer using a flex lease—base rent plus a percentage bonus calculated using a price/crop yield formula.

Steve and I married in 2005. In 2011, I was diagnosed with cervical/facial dystonia, which prevents me from working, so we decided to retire. We moved to the farm in June 2012. In 2004, we were already aware of how finite the Earth's resources are and how they are being overexploited, even depleted. As we contemplated our retirement, most popular locations—like Florida, Texas, Arizona, and Colorado—are hot and/or dry, characterized by high natural resources use and low sustainability. Our checklist for locations included land providing a local food source, abundant clean water, high sustainability, moderate seasonal climate, one to two hours from a major city, and a five- to eight-hour drive from Steve's three sons in Minneapolis.

Red Oak and my farm met these criteria. My farmland potentially could be very sustainable. This is the most fertile land in the world, and it has adequate water resources. There are railroads and navigable rivers nearby for transportation. When fossil fuels become scarce and expensive, mass transit availability will be important. Finally, we saw potential in the building site, which had been neglected for many years.

We decided the farmhouse, well-built in its day, could not be renovated to be highly energy efficient. We decided to build a new Passivhaus, a German design incorporating an airtight, highly insulated structure with passive solar energy gain. We finished the house in December 2014. Additionally, we installed a solar energy array in 2013, which generates about 40 percent of the electricity for the farm and house.

My top goal for the farm is to conserve and improve the sustainability of the farmland's use for the long term. Key to achieving this goal are conservation efforts, restoring native prairie, and employing sustainable farming practices. Some of my farmland has been in the Conservation Reserve Program (CRP) and Conservation Stewardship Program (CSP) since 1997. I just renewed contracts for both programs in 2013 and 2015.

I have two CRP plots: a grass waterway including native grasses and our newest project, a riparian buffer along our creek. In May 2015, we planted 1,500 trees and shrubs to extend the riparian buffer the full length of our creek. We killed the invasive reed canary grass in preparation for the planting. Now, native wetland plants such as arrowhead and milkweed are recolonizing. My oldest brother, who is a forestry consultant and conservationist, worked with us on this project.

Two plots planted as restored native prairie are CSP projects, while one restored native prairie plot is part of the Iowa State University (ISU) STRIPs program (a project that integrates row crops with strips of prairie in order to improve water quality and provide other benefits). We planted a pollinator native prairie plot next to our riparian buffer this month, and plan to add another ISU STRIPs plot in 2016.

Additional conservation plans include adding several grassy waterways rather than building more tiled terraces, and repairing two ponds.

Cover crops are another conservation and sustainability focus for us. In 2013 and 2015, we planted cover crops in tests plots and plan to increase our use of cover crops in future years. As a final note, I have a personal vendetta against invasive nonnative species. I am continually pulling weeds—thistles, smartweed, bindweed, multiflora rose, and horse nettles! Steve digs the poison ivy since I'm highly allergic.

My top goal for this farm is to conserve and improve the soil, increase biodiversity, improve water quality, and provide wildlife habitat. My long-term goal/dream is to have the farm be an educational resource for agricultural conservation and sustainability best practices, and be viewed as a role model (worthy cause). Also, I want the land to continue as a working farm for a family that embraces Steve's and my conservation and sustainability values.

The following goals are also important to me: to provide land for my heirs as a safe haven in event of a catastrophic situation in the USA, to maintain family harmony, and to reassemble the original 508 acres of my parents' farmland into a single farm.

STEVE TURMAN

I don't own the land here at Resilient Farms, but I am committed to Maggie and to the farm. My top goal for this land is to use it more sustainably, which includes conserving and improving soil, increasing biodiversity, improving water quality, and other measures. One critical reason for this is that I want to provide a place where family can survive, if necessary. Given the size of the property, this will require not dividing it and, if possible, acquiring adjacent land.

Another goal is to provide an example of sustainable land use, including how to transition from current use (typical corn-soybean rotation) to something that mimics nature more closely, and thus foster long-term productivity (our region evolved as tallgrass prairie/savanna that was regularly grazed and periodically burned).

I don't think our future involves a Hollywood-style apocalyptic scenario, but I do believe, given our addiction to economic growth with its attendant resource depletion and waste production (some of these depleting resources are not renewable, at least on a human time scale—fossil fuels and many critical minerals, for instance), we are degrading our biosphere in a way that harms the basis of human civilization and the web of life we take for granted. We are seeing that our biosphere has limits and that we are beginning to experience those; we are realizing that we cannot have our planet and eat it too, so to speak. One way or another, our future will include occupying this landscape differently than we have for the past few centuries.

As rational beings we can choose to make this transition deliberate, or we can deny realities, cling to our habits, and thus contribute to a likely chaotic and painful transition. Maggie and I may not live long enough to complete what we have started here, but with Resilient Farms, we have the opportunity to begin to make the changes necessary to survive, and hopefully thrive, in the future that awaits us.

Many Moments of Grace
by Fred Kirschenmann, Medina, North Dakota

My father and mother started farming in south-central North Dakota when they got married in 1930. They originally had 500 acres that they rented and eventually bought. As land became available, they added additional acres to the farm. When I moved back to the farm in 1976, the farm was 2,500 acres. We bought another three-quarter section after I started farming. At its largest, the farm was 3,500 acres, with approximately 900 acres of that in native prairies, used for animal grazing, and the rest cropped acres.

My parents' farm was highly diversified. We raised wheat, rye, and barley, plus oats to feed the horses. There was not a lot of alfalfa back then. We had beef cattle, ducks, guinea hens, chickens, and some pigs. We also had dairy for our own use and sold cream to a creamery in Bismarck. Our egg enterprise was my mother's; she used the income to buy groceries. Back then, you could take eggs into the grocery store to sell them.

The Dust Bowl, with its huge winds and soil erosion, had an enormous effect on the northern plains. My father somehow understood, intuitively, that the Dust Bowl was not just about the weather (which most of his neighbors assumed) but that it was also about the way farmers farmed. So he began to plant trees, and to keep fields relatively small and arranged in crop rotations so they were not as exposed to the wind. "It was Roosevelt who taught us how to farm because of his soil erosion programs," he said, even though he was a Republican!

After World War II, when fertilizers became available in North Dakota, my father started to hear about how they could increase yields. He was intrigued, since he wanted to be the best wheat farmer in Stutsman County, but his passion for taking care of the land worried him because he wondered if applying the fertilizer would hurt his soils. He talked to his county extension agent and other farmers whose judgment he valued, and everyone told him the fertilizer would just add nutrients, so he decided to start applying it. Wheat was the best cash crop, and adding fertilizer increased yields without crop rotations, so he started to raise more wheat. Then he had more weeds because of the reduced crop rotation. Then he started using herbicides to take care of the weeds.

My father was insistent I get as much education as I could, because he had been denied that. He only went through sixth grade, and he thought that if he had been allowed to go to school longer, he would have been a better farmer. So I got a Ph.D. and started a career in higher education. It was during those years that I met David Vetter, a Nebraska farmer and student of mine. He introduced me to organic agriculture. His passion was to get more people to manage their soils better. He showed me the difference between organically managed and conventionally managed soil, and how farming organically could improve soil health.

The first summer after I met David, I showed my father photos comparing conventional versus organic soils. "Now it's clear to me what the problem is," my dad said. "I've noticed that earthworms have been disappearing." A neighbor who had never bought into the fertilizer application scenario—instead he maintained a crop rotation that included yellow blossom sweet clover as a cover crop—had gotten ill and asked my father to rent his land from him on a crop-share basis, which required that my father keep the crop harvested from the neighbor's land separate. The test weight and protein levels of the wheat harvested from the neighbor's land were always higher than that harvested from our land. It had been an annoying mystery; now my father concluded that it had to be the difference in the quality of the soil.

So I asked my father if he would consider converting our farm to an organic farm. My dad was sixty-eight years old at the time and decided he was too old to take on an "altogether different kind of farming." In 1976, he had a mild heart attack, and his doctor said he could still be a farmer but that he had to get out of the stress of managing the farm. I spent some time with him during his recovery and asked him what he was going to do. He told me he was going to find someone to manage the farm for him. He was a Russian-German who had stern ideas, and I knew hiring a stranger to manage his farm for him was not likely to work out very well. I had a big organic garden and had done research on organic farming and became increasingly intrigued by the concept. So my family and I decided to leave higher education and return to North Dakota to convert the farm to an organic operation.

By the time I came back, my father, like most of his neighbors, had begun to specialize. Wheat was his major crop. He still had some sheep, but the animal part of the farm was mostly a cow-calf operation.

I started to make some changes, experimenting with diverse crop rotations. My neighbors thought I was going to take my father's farm from success to failure. Neighbors rarely tell you things directly, but they tell other neighbors. Eventually, their concerns were communicated to me. "His father worked so hard all his life to create a successful farm, and now his son is going to ruin it."

Initially, my crop rotation included wheat, winter rye, flax, buckwheat, millet, and alfalfa. It became clear early on that a legume in the rotation was essential. I fed the cattle the alfalfa during the winter months, and alfalfa plus the composted manure accumulated during the winter months restored the health of the soil for crop production. Later I added canola. I alternated cool- and warm-season crops to help suppress weeds and disease.

Nine hundred acres of the farm continue to be reserved as native prairie, which we use for grazing our animals from spring to fall. This is land that has never been plowed, and as long as I own it, it won't be.

During the first couple of years, while the croplands were transitioned to organic, the crops didn't always look that good. Once I figured out the rotation, my crops looked better or as good as the neighbors' crops did with fertilizer. Eventually, some neighbors became intrigued enough to explore farming organically for themselves. However, because government subsidies only applied to a few commodity crops and there were none for many of the crops essential to the rotation—plus the risks involved in the transition—most, understandably, never made the change.

My father's health continued to make it impossible for him to be fully engaged in the farming operation, so I hired a young man out of high school to join the farm, and he supplied some of the labor for several years. Eventually, he got married and decided to begin farming on his own.

I usually stopped by the local gas station, where Steve Sund worked, on Sundays. Steve was a tree surgeon but occasionally worked at the gas station as well. One Sunday, shortly after our hired help left the farm, Steve told me his father was retiring and his two older brothers both wanted to farm. His father had decided that their farm couldn't support all three sons. "I've always wanted to be a farmer, but now I can't be one," he said. So I said, "Steve, I have a farm." We talked, and within five minutes we had a deal. And Steve and his family joined our farm.

By July 2000, when I was invited to become the second director of the Leopold Center in Iowa, I was able to accept that opportunity because by then, Steve and his family were able to take over the farm's day-to-day operations.

Steve wouldn't be farming if he couldn't do it organically. His oldest son has now taken over the beef operation. The family also raises draft horses, quarter horses, and chickens. I always go up to North Dakota between Christmas and New Year's to file our farm's taxes, and sometimes we go out to dinner together. One year, during dinner, Steve's six-year-old son told me he was especially excited about their donkeys. I said, "Donkeys?" He said, "Yes, and we sell them on the Internet to sheep ranchers in the western Dakotas for predator control."

When my father planned his estate, he operated on the assumption that our farm was a "family farm" and would always remain a family farm, and he put the farm in my sister's and my name equally. He also requested that if we both decided some day to quit farming, he wanted the land to go to his grandchildren. But when my sister turned eighty, she decided she wanted out, so we had to partition the farm four years ago. My current portion is about 1,900 acres, and the 900 acres of native prairie still belong to me.

A lesson I learned in this process is that one should never operate on assumptions. If I had not assumed that my sister would always remain part of the farm, we would have developed a plan for ownership transition: in case one of us wants to get out, what is our plan for doing that? But we didn't, so we had problems.

The good news, from my perspective, is that once the farm was reduced in size, Steve said, "I think we could take it over now." They aren't in a position to, nor want to, buy the land and the buildings, but they are in the process of buying the equipment and starting to make all of the operation decisions. They continue to maintain it as an organic, biodynamic farm.

I treat Steve like family. To make this transition successfully, both he and I recognize that we need to really want to do this and work together to come up with creative and practical transition proposals. If either of us decided we only were doing it for the money, it would never work.

In the last twenty-five years, a number of things have happened that influenced what we can grow on our farm. Sunflowers are a warm-season leafy crop that fit perfectly into the crop rotation in our part of North Dakota. But we had to give up sunflowers because of blackbird predation. When all of our neighbors also raised sunflowers, the blackbirds were dispersed among all of our fields, and we could all live with some loss. But as seed companies started to produce earlier maturing varieties of corn and soybeans, and government subsidies for corn and beans far exceeded any subsidies for wheat and sunflowers, farmers quit growing sunflowers, and consequently the blackbirds were all in my fields. As a result, by the mid-1990s, when I was the only farmer in our neighborhood who was still growing sunflowers, I began to lose 60 percent of my sunflower crop to the birds.

We also had to give up canola. Canola is, of course, an insect-pollinated crop, and when our neighbors started planting Roundup Ready canola, a two-mile buffer was required to prevent cross-pollination. Our neighbors were always respectful of our farming methods, and they would always tell me where they were going to plant their canola, and we could plant ours in the rotation at least two miles from their fields. However, eventually Roundup Ready canola became so popular there was no way to achieve a two-mile buffer. Nineteen ninety-three was the last year we raised canola. That change resulted in a $50,000 annual loss in income to our farm, since there was a co-op in our area that processed our canola into organic canola oil, which was in huge demand in California.

Buckwheat was always an important crop in our rotation. Early on, almost all of our organic grains were exported to Europe. Now we sell mostly in the United States. But buckwheat has never been used much as a food crop in the United States. European farmers apparently figured out they could raise buckwheat for the markets in Europe, so it has become difficult to market buckwheat.

So now the basic crops on my farm are winter rye, hard red spring wheat, some barley, golden flax, and alfalfa. Our biodynamic golden flax is still in big demand in Europe, but in 2014 our flax sample contained .075 glyphosate contamination, and the tolerance level is zero in Europe, which was my market. So we lost that market. Fortunately, we have been able to find a market for organic golden flax in the United States, where tolerance levels are higher. But it is probably only a matter of time before contamination is higher than tolerance levels in the United States as well. Since we currently get more than a 50 percent premium for organic golden flax compared to conventional prices, that will be another serious loss to our farm.

I love the principle of coexistence. I believe that all farmers should be free to farm the way they want and that we all cooperate and that organic and conventional farming should be compatible. But you can't fence out a part of nature, so there will increasingly be a problem.

For me, the core value instilled in me by my father continues to be what guides my farming decisions. I can still see my father lecturing me when I was five years old, reminding me that "taking care of land is more important than making money, more important than anything else." Years later, filmmakers created a video about our farm called *My Father's Garden*. One of the scenes in that video was of my father and me standing behind a field cultivator. He was looking at the soil, pointing out how porous and rich it was, and reminding me that if the way we farmed now produced such soil, then that was all that mattered. Such moments continue to be significant for me.

My principal goal is that my farm be farmed like nature. I want my farm to be regenerative and resilient so that the soil's synergies are renewed and the resilient properties of biodiversity are increased. My ecologic goals are more important than economic ones. If the farm is not regenerative, it will not be economically viable, especially when all of the cheap inputs on which agriculture has become dependent become depleted.

I prefer that the farmland is owned by my family in the future. But my ecologic goal trumps this wish.

I am abiding by the wishes of my father, and the land is being transferred to my son and daughter. They share my values, and they want it farmed organically as well. Indeed, the quarter section where my daughter is has already been transferred to her.

Can a case be made for a conservation easement on my farm? If there were any doubt of the values of my children, I would go in that direction. But when you make decisions based on the current understanding of reality, you may not get to your end result fifty years from now. It was much more important to have the passion and commitment of my children.

One of my passions now is to try and think about sustainability and the design of our future agricultural and food systems. As challenging as some of the transition from conventional to organic is, that transition is simple compared to the challenges farmers are going to face when crude oil is $300 a barrel and rock phosphate, essential to conventional farmers, is $2,500 a ton rather than the $700 a ton it is now. By most estimates, we only have about twenty years of rock phosphate reserves left in the United States. We are depleting our freshwater resources, and our climate is becoming more unstable. On my North Dakota farm, Steve and I are thinking about these challenges and how we can have a farm that is "sustainable" twenty years from now. We cannot operate by the old playbook.

In *The Great Work*, Thomas Berry reminds us that moments of crisis are always moments of grace. We tend not to make changes until we feel the pain of our current operations. I suspect we will have a lot of moments of grace in our future! I am not that worried about my farm going non-organic with future generations. As energy and input costs increase, the way it is farmed now will be practical. As Sir Albert Howard reminded us almost eighty years ago, when we farm in nature's image we will realize that Mother Earth never attempts to farm without livestock; she always raises mixed crops; great pains are taken to preserve the soil and to prevent erosion; the mixed vegetable and animal wastes are converted into humus; there is no waste; the processes of growth and the processes of decay balance one another; ample provision is made to maintain large reserves of fertility; the greatest care is taken to store the rainfall. This is the approach on my farm, and, I suspect, it will be on others' as well.

The Importance of Mentors
by Jeff Klinge and Deb Tidwell,
Farmersburg, Iowa

JEFF KLINGE

I grew up in this house near Farmersburg in northeast Iowa. The original 1899 farmhouse was twice the size, but that was just too much to heat, so my parents built this new one in 1947. Our basement is the original limestone rock formation from under the original house, and my dad incorporated the flooring and other things from the original house into this one.

I own 240 acres outright, and Deb and I own another 80 acres. We have always had crop rotation on this farm. When I was growing up, we had three years of corn and then a small grain and alfalfa. Now my land is certified organic, and you can't have the same crop two years in a row except perennials like alfalfa.

Back in the early 1980s, my dad started gifting us four boys stock in the farming corporation he set up for the 750-acre family farm. Three of us farm; my fourth brother basically sold out his share to my dad. That gifting lowered our debt when we bought the farmland. My dad also set the sale price on the farmland about as low as he could allow without running into the gift tax. Land wasn't so expensive back then either (this happened about the time of the Farm Crisis).

When my parents were in their late fifties, they bought long-term health care insurance. As they got older, they used these policies and didn't have to dip into any of the net worth of their estate. When my dad and mother passed away, we boys were beneficiaries of the life insurance they had purchased, which we used to pay off our loans on the farms. My dad was so thoughtful about this. People say life insurance isn't a good investment, but it sure paid off for this family. Between the life insurance, the gifting of the stock, and pricing the farm low, that made it easy for us boys.

When I think about growing up and living in rural Iowa, there are so many different things that come to mind.

One of my fondest memories was being with my grandparents on my mother's side. They lived on a small farm and used a wood-burning cookstove. Next to the cookstove was a woodbox with a door that had an outside entrance and an entrance into the house. When I was a real little kid, I would go outside, into the woodbox, and then come out inside the house. That just amazed the hell out of me.

My grandparents raised red Duroc hogs, and my brothers and I would chase the hogs into a little pen. One of my brothers would play like the auctioneer, and we would bid on them. We were just little farts at the time, but it was really fun.

My grandparents and aunt and uncle took us fishing quite a bit. It was great being able to grow up fishing on the Mississippi.

My mother always raised leghorn roosters. You could buy them for next to nothing at that time. They would roost in the grove, and we boys would have to climb up the trees at night and catch them. One time we were missing chickens, and we knew a fox was getting them. My dad was determined to stay up all night to get that fox. I waited with him, but then couldn't stay awake and went to bed about 1 a.m. Just as the sun was coming up, the fox came in through the field there on a dead run, and Dad got him with a shotgun.

We used to have some major snowstorms. One time when I was nine or ten, the neighbor kids got stranded here for several days, even though they only lived about 2.5 miles away. Some of the dairymen were digging tunnels in the snowdrifts to get their cows in and out of the barn. The county couldn't get the snow plowed, so they hired all the contractors around the region to clean the county roads.

When I was in my early twenties, here on the home farm we had avian tuberculosis in our hogs. One packing plant condemned a whole lot of them. One of the neighbors told Dad to try a different packing plant because the plants don't have the same inspectors. So we went to a different plant and got a whole bunch through. Then that plant started condemning them. The state veterinarian came out and thought the disease was brought in by birds; then they thought it was brought in by rodents. I asked a vet what was wrong with the hogs, and he said they had to be condemned because they had spots on the liver. "Is the meat fit to eat?" I asked. He said yes, and I said, "Why can't we go down to the plant and get some home to eat?" But once they were condemned, the rule was they couldn't leave the plant. What a waste. Why didn't they just throw the damn liver away?

As quick as the avian tuberculosis came in, all of a sudden we didn't have it anymore, and we never proved where it came from. None of our neighbors had it. Yes, that was a significant time for this farm.

I enjoyed farrowing hogs. I ended up with the farm that had the cattle feeding set up, and that's probably why I became a cattle feeder. My brother John lives across the field, and that place has the farrowing house and most of the hog finishing buildings. Baling hay and filling the barn with square bales was something we did as a family, and that continued after I grew up. It started off that my dad would load the bales on the wagon. As we got older, he drove the baler or did something else, and then we boys did the loading.

In the 1950s and early '60s, when we sent the cattle by semi to the Union Stock Yard in Chicago, we would catch a train in Prairie du Chien—they still had a station back then—and we would watch the cattle sell, then take in a baseball game. How great life could be! Well, the stockyards closed in Chicago about 1965. For a while, we had packing plants closer to the cattle, but now we haul them to eastern Colorado, which is between 800 and 900 miles. So Chicago was not far at all by comparison.

There were a few times when Dad and Mom bought calves right off the cow and brought them here from central Nebraska. When we put them in a feedlot, not only did they not have Mama but they were suddenly forced to eat feed and had very different water. They were really bawling. And it was always in the fall of the year, when it's rainy. It tends to be drier in central Nebraska than Iowa, so they'd get respiratory problems. I haven't bought bawling calves since I've had a business. You pay a lot more for feeders when they've been weaned. There is an animal welfare rule (in the natural program we use now) that says they need to be weaned forty-five days before being sold, which is a good rule. And for my system, they should be bunk broken, which means familiar with eating out of a feed bunk rather than just eating grass off the ground. If they never ate out of the feed bunk before, that's a big change too.

One cattle mishap I remember well happened in the early '60s, near Guttenberg. A car pulled out in front of a semi loaded with our cattle. The truck rolled over into a pond to try to avoid hitting the car. Some of the cattle drowned, and the rest got out and were running around Guttenberg. They managed to get them penned up again, I guess, but what a deal.

When I started working with cattle on my own, I lost so much money on the first group of cattle I owned, and it affected me for years to come. Then I fed Holsteins for fifteen years. I had some about ready to go the week the federal dairy buyout program came about. The government said, "Don't worry, this isn't going to affect the price," so I sent some to sale down in Tama that week, and my Holsteins dropped about 25 cents a hundredweight.

The last fifteen years, I have been feeding cattle for the Laura's Lean Beef program, but that has now been discontinued, so I am going to have to find other markets for my beef and possibly switch breeds. So many markets I know are going toward grass-fed beef, which doesn't work for me.

We've lost a lot of young farmers in this region of northeast Iowa, southwest Wisconsin, and southeast Minnesota. We started seeing significant change even with the Conservation Reserve Program (CRP). There were a lot of young dairy farmers who started out on the roughest land, because that was cheapest and no one else wanted to farm it. When the CRP came in, their landlord could make more money by putting their land in the CRP than by renting it to young dairy farmers. The idea of the CRP, as I understand it, was to take some of the lower-quality land out of production and by doing so help to lower the surplus and raise the overall price of grain. The irony of the program is that these beginning dairy farmers never added to the surplus but were forced out of farming so that the grain farmers on the better land could continue to make a living just growing row crops. So here's a program that is supposed to help farmers, but it resulted in a loss of beginning farmers. The CRP sure didn't help beginning farmers.

We should have more farmers, not fewer. Almost every farm program we've had has led to continuous row crop production of a few commodities and more concentration of ownership and businesses.

Ethanol and subsidized crop insurance make corn and soybean farmers more profitable, but at what cost to everybody else? If we didn't have farm programs just for the farmers who specialize in those two crops, the price of land could fall by as much as 50 percent. The big landowners would be crying something terrible, but it would be a shot in the arm for beginning farmers if they only had to pay half as much for land. If my land were worth half as much as it is, it wouldn't bother me that much. High land prices are only good for somebody who's using farmland as an investment to make money and not for the people who are actually trying to make a living farming it.

How do I want to be remembered in thirty years? That I got my giant ragweed under control. (Laughs.) I want my kids to remember how much they enjoyed coming here. I hope they had good memories of when they were growing up. They talk like they did anyway. Deb's not their birth mother, but she's been real good with them. And they really appreciate her, and that means a lot to me.

My top goal is to keep family harmony, to foster positive relationships among family members. Family comes first; close second is land. That's what's most important. I want to use the farmland to conserve and improve the soil, increase biodiversity, improve water quality, and other conservation. There's only so much land out there. Ever since I was a young child, I didn't like to see soil going down the river.

It is my duty as a farmer, as a human being, to try to leave this farm as good as or better than when I came. With my crop rotation, I hope the organic matter, the soil microbiology, is increasing.

I would like to see my farmland stay together, but if my kids aren't going to farm it and there's an opportunity to get more farmers making a profit on smaller pieces of land, that's fine. I would like to provide land for my farming heirs to farm, but I don't think my children are interested in actually living here and farming the land. If they are interested in keeping the land, that sounds good, but what happens after their generation? Are any grandchildren I have going to feel attached and committed to this?

I would like to give all of my heirs an inheritance of equal economic value, but if one of them wants to farm, I wouldn't be opposed to giving them some breaks that the other two don't have. I want to provide a farm for a family to work. I'm not going to sell to an investor, and if my children sell it, I'd rather they sell it to a family that works it (and doesn't own six or seven other farms). I don't know how much control I will have over that.

I want to end with the importance of mentors. I didn't always get along with my dad, but he was a very good mentor. People like [PFI cofounder] Dick Thompson, my close friend Dan Specht, and my brothers were mentors. Deb has been very important in my life. I have a tendency to get down on myself when things aren't going right. She lets me know I'm my own worst enemy.

DEB TIDWELL

I grew up in the San Francisco Bay area, and this northeast Iowa farm is very different. Before I met Jeff twenty-two years ago, I never lived in a place that had so much open space. I always lived in large communities, so I thought Denver was small when I moved to Denver. Then I moved to Tucson and thought, "So now, this is small." Then I became a professor at the University of Northern Iowa, and Cedar Falls was even smaller. And then I came to Farmersburg and this farm and thought, "I get it now—this is truly small." But I liked it. I downsized gradually.

I have developed a love for things like the county fair, which I'd never experienced before meeting Jeff. For example, if you bake like crazy and bring seven items, you can get a free armband. If you just grab a handful of wildflowers and put them in a vase, you might even get second place. (Laughs.) I also bring to the farm enthusiasm and an amazing appreciation for farmers and this farming life. I've watched these professional farmers use a lot of critical thinking to make their farms work. I find that very exciting. I've learned so much listening to Jeff and our friend Dan Specht talk about their farms.

I appreciate the longevity of five generations on this farm. When you live on a farm all of your life, it is what it is. But I think I helped Jeff see how amazing it is. There's such a history here that is just taken for granted.

My top goal for our farmland is to use it to conserve or improve soil, increase biodiversity, improve water quality, and other conservation. Without these, nothing else can happen. You cannot farm when your soil has become a biological wasteland, and I'm really getting concerned about the next generation's water quality.

My secondary goals are to provide a farm for a family to work and to provide land for my farming heirs to farm. I wish these two would go together. It would be ideal to give my heirs an inheritance of equal economic value. All three kids enjoy the farm so much.

Jeff has worked hard his entire life creating this environment where we all can get along. With the children living off the farm, Jeff has pulled this all together because he is family-centered. He talks to the kids (Noah, Elizabeth, and Christina) every week by cell phone or email, whether they are in Phoenix, Des Moines, even Germany. Jeff and I both believe in the importance of family harmony—we work at creating a farm home environment that enables Noah, Elizabeth, and Christina to feel connected. We've really wanted this farm to be a safe place where the kids can come because it's their home too.

I really don't care if the farmland stays together; it depends on what the kids want to do with it. If the kids want to break it up into four vegetable farms, or if they want to keep the prairie and have this be the home farm when they come, I'm fine with that.

I think Jeff sees this farm as part of a larger community. This farm, the markets, and the local community are all connected. Every aspect of the farm is important to him. Even the choices he made that you see right out this window. He chose the right trees and location, and this beautiful canopy that has developed over twenty-five years is the result. It cools the house, which lowers energy costs, but it also provides habitat for the birds. You walk out in our yard, and it's a cacophony of noise in the morning. It makes for a very pleasant homestead.

I like the idea of a presumption of competence. When you get challenges, you just presume that you can solve the challenges. It's just a matter of finding the right path. It might take five years, but we can get there. Like this giant ragweed problem. We're going to get it under control.

Instead of Jeff being remembered as the guy with the ragweed problem, I'd like him to be remembered as the guy who really did appreciate land not just because of what it did for him, but what he did for it. He not only survived on this farm, he made it thrive.

Make Us an Offer

by Teresa Opheim

In the early 1990s, Martha Shivvers Skillman started looking around for a more sustainable farmer to work the land she had inherited with her sisters near Knoxville, Iowa. She was told not to get her hopes up. Farmers who might have been interested "were wiped out in the '80s," people told her. That was the wrong thing to tell Martha, who, like her sisters, is of determined and resourceful stock.

Jump to early 2009, when farmer Jim Petersen of Knoxville purchased 160 acres from Martha and her sisters to help his young adult sons start farming. How did the two families come together to make the land transfer that needs to happen a thousand times over if we are to have a future of diverse farms and vibrant communities?

Martha Skillman and her sisters, Charlotte Shivvers and Marietta Carr, grew up on the family's farm, but all left in the 1940s after finishing high school, Martha to Chicago as an occupational therapist, then into horticulture. Charlotte was a teacher, then realtor, then Unitarian Universalist minister around the country. Marietta moved west and became a medical administrator.

For all three, though, the pull of farm and family was strong.

"I was always coming back to Iowa, mainly to visit Mother, particularly when all those trains used to run back and forth from Chicago," Martha says. Their father, John, died in 1962, and their mother died in 1990. Then the sisters had the great fortune to inherit 520 acres of good Iowa land, to agree that they wanted to keep it, and to form a partnership they named Shivvers Fair Acres.

"I took over as our sisters' first managing partner," Martha said. "Then, in the early 1990s, I moved back to Iowa into the little house here that was originally used to house the hired man." Charlotte and her husband, Bob Baker, moved back to the farm in 1996. They now live in the original farmhouse, and Charlotte is the current managing partner.

There is a large web of Shivvers all over south-central Iowa, aunts and uncles, nieces and nephews, first and second cousins. These three sisters are descended from Celly (Marcellus) and Molly Mills Shivvers, who bought the farm in 1903, complete with a big red barn labeled "Fair Acres 1882." The girls' father was the youngest of their eight children and got the homeplace.

There is an annual Shivvers picnic to help the family stay connected, and it was at this picnic during the Farm Crisis of the 1980s that Charlotte visited with her cousin-in-law Folmer Petersen. Folmer told Charlotte that he was in serious financial trouble and about to lose the home farm that his son, Jim, so wanted to farm. Charlotte listened and suggested that they try for a loan from her mother, Vera. Marietta advised their cousin Norma, Folmer's wife, the same way. And Vera Shivvers got to express her passion for the family farm by loaning the necessary dollars to Folmer's son, Jim.

"We got to know Jim and his wife, Julie, that way. They never missed the opportunity to thank us, and Jim paid the loan back just as agreed," Martha says. "Then I discovered that Jim was trying different farming methods that we hadn't been able to get our farm operators to do." The Petersens and Shivvers started to talk. The Shivvers heard more about the Petersen farming approach and that the two older boys, Justin and Jacob, were interested in organic agriculture.

The sisters agreed that they would like to rent 160 acres to the Petersens to be farmed organically. Managing partner Charlotte sought advice and then worked out with the Petersens a lease whereby landlord and tenant shared the risks and yet had a cash rent arrangement. They learned about organic together.

Perhaps the hardest part, Martha said, was "another set of cousins, good conventional farmers, had been farming that land, and we had to take it from them. That was a painful process. But they hadn't done what we asked for, and we were serious about trying more eco-friendly farming."

The Petersens began renting the land in 2004. Early each December, Jim would report how the money had been spent and the income that was coming in. His father, Folmer, a longtime soil and water conservation district commissioner in Marion County, continued to help out. "He was particularly helpful in identifying and augmenting tile drainage lines," Martha said. "The Petersens educated us about our land in a way that no one else had since our father's death." And the arrangement worked financially for all concerned.

Jim eventually got up the nerve to ask the Shivvers if they would consider a sale of the land he was renting. Marietta, Martha, and Charlotte explored with their children how they would feel about parting with a portion of the farm. "Each of those children responded: 'I love the farm, but I won't be coming back,'" reported Martha. "Our kids were open to Jim's request because they liked the kind of farming he was doing, and like their parents, they wanted a way for the farm to continue as sustainable."

Charlotte told Jim, "Make us an offer on the 160 acres you rent." About two years later he did. "Practical Farmers' Next Generation meetings taught me to get out and do something about getting more land. Don't wait," Jim says. It was actually easy to agree on a price; Jim's banker named a number that he thought Jim could handle without having to mortgage his home. And, as Marietta said, "We don't want that to happen." The 160 acres went for below market value, but there were restrictions placed in the contract in an attempt to assure good stewardship through the years.

"The most assurance comes from the fact that we trust the Petersens to farm in a way that puts care of land first," Charlotte said.

In 2014, the Shivvers sisters sold the Petersens another 40 acres of farmland. Marietta Shivvers Carr died in July 2015, and her active part in Fair Acres decision making was taken over by her daughter, Melissa Carr-Buswell, who, together with four other Shivvers offspring, will inherit the Shivvers sisters' remaining farmland. The Petersens now farm all of the Shivvers' land and have added the land into their five-year crop rotation and rotational grazing system.

Jim continues to farm full time with oldest son Justin, who has followed in his grandfather's footsteps by serving as a commissioner of the soil and water conservation district. Son Jacob works full time with his father. He bought a farm nearby and, with his wife, Lauren, is moving into the production of sheep milk for cheese. Son Josh uses part of the Petersen homeplace property to manage his own machinery repair business—and is available when needed for farming. Daughter Jenny has won many sheep awards as well as scholarships and is now at Iowa State University majoring in agricultural communication with a minor in animal science.

One summer after the first land sale, Jim, Martha, and Charlotte took some time to sit on Charlotte's front porch swing, which overlooks the now-Petersen land off to the southeast. One sister smiled as she told Jim, "We three sisters could argue about how much to spend for dinner, but we were in complete agreement about this sale." Later she adds, "We can joke now, but early on our differences weren't funny. We found a social worker attuned to family business issues and got help."

All Who Went Before
by Jim and Lisa French, Partridge, Kansas

JIM FRENCH

I am the fifth generation on our farm, located in Reno County, south-central Kansas. Richard Calverley was my maternal ancestor who first farmed; he emigrated from England in 1852. In 1872, he homesteaded our farm with his wife, Mary. The original dugout is still part of the basement my nephew lives in!

Over the last forty to fifty years, our farm has had primarily a cow-calf operation and cash crops such as wheat and grain sorghum. In the last six years, we have grown soybeans. We also have alfalfa and have used cover crops since 1983. We have gone away from mono cover crops and now do blends—one legume, one brassica, and one grass. We've become really interested in soil quality and soil health.

We are always on the learning curve, trying new things and taking advantage of opportunities.

My early memories include sitting on my father's lap on an International Farmall trying to learn to pull a small farm field cultivator and not leave a gap between the previous pass. I was probably eight or so. We had a chicken yard. We'd get the chicks in the mail in the spring. My mother told stories about butchering three chickens a day for the crews coming through. When I was growing up, Dad also had farrowing sows.

I was a free-range child. When Dad would go to the field in the summertime, he'd sometimes drop me off at the creek with a can of worms and a fishing pole. I'd spend the morning catching perch and catfish and enjoying myself. The sound of his tractor would be close by. We rode our bikes everywhere with the neighbor kids. There was always a neighbor close by, and we knew parents were watching us.

From the age of fourteen I worked quite a bit with my father. As I went through college and grad school, I would come home in the summer to farm. I only missed one summer on the farm in my whole life!

When my father was sixty-four, he was having trouble with his back. My wife, Lisa, and I had an opportunity to come and take over the farm when he hit sixty-five. We love the rural area and communities, so we moved back full time in June 1979. The first thing we did was purchase a Buffalo no-till planter. I still use that planter.

When I came back, I was an idealistic young farmer full of [the author] Wendell Berry. My father was more practical and made sure we could make a living. For Lisa and me, almost all of our decisions stem back to how we can best serve the land, how we can be good stewards. But we had to make sure we were economically responsible so that we could continue.

At one time, we thought about organic, but we became convinced that in order to become organic we'd give up on other goals, like limiting tillage. Limited and no-till with cover crops decreased our chemical usage.

From October 1992 to May 1993, we witnessed our first big climate extreme. I ended up with 25 acres of grain sorghum that we could not get harvested because it was so wet. Our calving peak was the first week of February, and the mud was so deep and the work so hard. I was constantly in emergency mode during that time, just trying to hold things together. We came through pretty well financially, but I lost about thirty pounds, was exhausted, and got quite sick. We had made ourselves very vulnerable, because we were calving at the wrong time of year. It was a wake-up call to be more resilient.

We were able to buy land in the '80s and early '90s, and got that paid off by 2005. My parents passed away, and we inherited more land there. Today we own 350–400 acres, and I am managing 500 acres total. I have a voice in how my cousin farms another 600–700 acres. We hire quite a bit of labor now, and we look for people to hire who have a similar interest in soil quality and rotational grazing.

Through the years, I have loved working with children through 4-H. For a while, I was the 4-H beef and parliamentary procedure leader in our local club. Our two children had calves and chickens, and I also work with other kids. It is terrific going to the fair and seeing them take pride in what they did.

Lisa and I farmed full time through 1998, but then we felt like we didn't have the income to support ourselves and two college-age youngsters, so we both started working off the farm. We rented out part of the farm for the first time in 2005. We decided we didn't need to have all of our income based on farming. My great-grandfather was a shoemaker; Lisa's was a mechanic. They were diversified. Others worked part-time jobs in town. Others consolidated and got bigger to be viable.

I feel blessed by my off-farm work with the Kansas Rural Center and Oxfam America. Lisa heads up a water quality project. We both feel like we can take our values we have about rural life, communities, and small-scale producers forward onto a broader stage and also feel like we are serving our community as well. We are not just producing crops and livestock on this farm; we are preserving rural values.

How can we go ahead and find a way to bring this land together and have it as a unit to pass on in the future? Our land is spread over more than three miles. One pasture is farther away, and we'd like to swap that for something closer. Around here, having a farm all in one place is fairly rare.

My top goal for my farmland is to use the land to conserve or improve soil, increase biodiversity, improve water quality. Without conservation and soil quality, there won't be a foundation to support other goals. There is more to consider for the future beyond my family. There are the other residents of the land: wildlife, plants, and the full picture of biodiversity. These goals are also my priorities: I would like to keep our farmland together as a coherent unit. I would like to provide land for my farming heirs to farm. If a family member wants to continue to farm and meet our conservation goals, then that should happen. If not, I would like to find someone in the community to do that. I would like to keep family harmony and foster positive relationships among my family members.

I am not as concerned if my children don't want to come back to farm, because I'm reinforcing my values in the community I live in. I hope I can have a community where kids can ride their bikes, enjoy nature, and have clean water. That's our vision for rural America.

I love to hear the sounds of the sandhill cranes when they migrate, usually in March. To see the windbreaks, the trees, and the native grasses on our farm, and the way we have tried to imitate nature in our pastures and grassland really appeals to me.

When we sit out on the deck at night, sipping our glasses of wine, we see our heritage and all who went before us. There is something so valuable in that continuity, embedded in the past and our vision we want to see in the future.

LISA FRENCH

I grew up five miles from where I live now. After I married Jim, we went to college and were out of state for a few years. We came back to the farm in 1979, even though Jim's parents didn't really encourage it. I worked in town for a while. When we had a family, I decided to stay home for a number of years.

Our two children are both attorneys in Kansas City, and we have one grandchild. I don't think either of our children will farm, but they both have affection for the farm.

When we came back, Jim's family had cattle in a conventional grazing pattern: take them to the pasture in the spring and pick them up in the fall. They also had wheat, milo, and alfalfa. We still have a cow-calf operation, but we've moved to a smaller number of animals grazed throughout the year. We try to incorporate the cattle into all aspects of the farm, including grazing native grasses and other kinds of forage. We market some for grass-fed beef, some commercially, and some as replacements. We still have wheat and sorghum that is sold off the farm. We do have hay production, but we think that's about to end. Over the years, we have converted about 100 acres from field crops to grazing.

When I am out on the farm, I see things I don't see when driving down the road: the different animals, the birds, the way the weather rolls through, the changing of the seasons. I especially notice things if I am outside by myself for a long time during the day. The connections we make with the natural world are very strong. All who work on the farm know this.

I remember teaching our kids to drive before they were technically old enough to drive. We would take them to the middle of the field so there was not much they could do wrong! I remember building fence with them and some 4-H projects with chickens that they did. Jim has been really good to work with kids raising 4-H calves. He still does that, calling them up to see how they're doing.

I have strong memories of walking through the rangeland, trying to identify particular plants. And the weather extremes—incredibly hot days in the summer, on the opposite day extreme cold when you still have to keep equipment going and check on animals. Years of drought, years of flooding.

I remember the smell when we're working the ground and the smell of hay and the manure in moist air. Cattle have their own particular pleasant scent. All the crops have their own smells. Wild plants like poison hemlock have such a strong scent. There is a definite smell in butchering chickens!

We have had lots of wonderful parties on the farm. We were part of a group of farmers who did cooperative chicken butchering and other projects. We all had kids in grade school at the time. I'd like to connect back with that again.

My negative memories are when things fell apart. Machinery breakdowns would happen when we just weren't paying enough attention. One time we were trying to unhitch something, and it flipped in the air and flipped Jim as well. He came out okay, but that memory sticks with me. There is such danger in farming! We don't often hear the difficult things about farming when we hear this "praise the farmer" talk.

Nineteen ninety-three was an extremely wet year. We were still trying to calve in a lot. Jim should have been in the hospital, he was so sick. My sister and I were trying to doctor calves, and neither of us is good with needles. We were up to our knees in mud, and walking right out of our boots.

The most positive thing we've done here is improve the soil. We have used Holistic Management to build conservation on this farm. Our system of moving cattle around is so intricate. We do things differently than most of the neighbors, so we are always searching for the right person to hire for the farm. We'd like someone to take over who recognizes the value of this management system. It would be a shame to lose the improvements in soil and habitat!

We are at an interesting point where we are not ready to leave our other jobs, but we are thinking about how that would work. It produces a lot of thoughts about finances, our land, what farming we're going to do in the future. We are working on increasing our nonland investments because a lot of our wealth is tied up in land.

Here is a conversation we need to have with our children: Should we sell part of our land? Will we have to? There may be some need to do so for their stability and for ours. We have just gone through the process of creating a trust. Every dime and piece of property we have could be needed to take care of us until we die. You wonder how all that is going to work out. That hangs over you a bit.

How can we preserve some of what we have done to make a healthy system while still recognizing we may have financial needs? Maybe the financial stability for us will come when our children, other relatives, or another family purchases some of our land. I don't want to see it go to auction where we have no control over to whom it's going to go!

One of the neighbors referred to Jim as "Mr. Hodge Podge." We have a diverse system. We make do with the machinery we have. Maybe that's a good term for us. We want people to remember that we were involved with our community. We partnered with other farmers, both near and far. Integrating the arts—music and literature—with farming has been important to us. We're probably looked at as outside of the mainstream. People think that we aren't doing things the most efficiently and maximizing profit. We will probably be known more for participation in the wider community rather than just the local farming community.

I am really heartened by the emphasis these days on soil health and cover crops. We've worked a long time on this, but now it's becoming more mainstream. No-till and organic farmers are starting to talk the same things—fewer chemicals. But they are coming at it from different directions. It's really encouraging. Farmers have a sense of stewardship, but for many that can mean a tidy field, lots of tillage, and continuous wheat. That is a much different view of stewardship than when you have diverse cropping and bring livestock into the system.

My number one goal for my farmland is to conserve and improve the soil, increase biodiversity, improve water quality, and other conservation. These are the most important things that we can do, regardless of who is farming the land.

My goals are also to provide my heirs with financial stability and to provide a farm for a family to farm. This land is probably the primary "thing" that we will leave. I would like to see our heirs or another family tending and conserving it and earning a living.

A Tribute to Dan Specht

18

One Man's Meat *by Teresa Opheim*

Dan Specht, a McGregor farmer, conservationist, and beloved member of Practical Farmers of Iowa, died in 2013 in an accident on his farm. He left behind hundreds of friends, family, and admirers—and also boxes of his beef. I bought a couple of those boxes, and soon schemed up a way to honor Dan's memory: gifts of meat to a chosen few who are continuing his work for an agriculture that is good for people and for the land.

I put a couple packages of minute steak in the vegetable box I returned to one of "my farmers," Julia Slocum of Lacewing Acres. Julia is a beginning farmer growing vegetables, Dan's product was beef, but both faced that uphill battle of farming profitability without government support given freely to those raising corn and soybeans.

I dropped off a roast with Matt Liebman, a professor at Iowa State University. Dan worked, as Matt does, to implement a vision of an agriculture that would ensure our future. Both delight (delighted) in the complexities of ecology as a model for agriculture and lamented the ignorance and lack of respect for the soil that we wash away at our peril.

Musician and agronomist Rick Exner got a roast for his musical talent with the band The Porch Stompers. Dan so enjoyed music (and the beer that often went with it). At a 2013 memorial concert held in northeast Iowa, musician Jon Stravers said that Dan had been the band's best fan. I thought the same thing about Dan and Practical Farmers of Iowa—there was no one who came to as many events.

A former staffer of Practical Farmers, Tomoko Ogawa, accepted a gift of Dan's steak. As our staff cook, she did her best to honor farmers through preparation of their food. Tomoko, who is not a native English speaker, wrote a poignant tribute about Dan after his death: "Dan always asked me for advice about how to cook a meal for his field day. I'm sure he cared about and loved good food and drink, but I think he was doing this in part because he knew that food was the language I feel fully competent to speak. He had that kind of genuine sensitivity and kindness."

And then I came home and enjoyed a meal with my family of spaghetti with Dan's ground beef flavoring the home-canned tomatoes.

The last of gifts, bones for soup, were delivered right out my back door to my dogs Liz and Maggie. They gnawed away on the bones for hours and perhaps savored the gift of Dan's labors most of all.

I am grateful for the opportunity to know the individual farmers who grow much of my food. I can empathize with them and their trials with both extreme floods and extreme drought all in one year, and the problems of finding enough consumers to pay them the price they need to make a living. I can celebrate their vocation with every meal I have. And then I have the bittersweet gift of mourning them when they are taken from us.

One man's meat.

One connection between a farmer and eater is now completed.

My Responsibility Now *by Mary Damm*

I met Dan at the 2004 North American Tallgrass Prairie Conference in Madison, Wisconsin. We were on a field trip to a hill prairie along the Wisconsin River, and he made the comment to me that "this looks like my farm in Iowa." I said: "In Iowa?" I was surprised, because I didn't think of Iowa as beautiful and rolling like this prairie bluff landscape. That evening there was a barbeque, and Dan introduced me to Laura Jackson, a biologist at the University of Northern Iowa. After the prairie conference was over, I went to a used bookstore in Madison and found a book that Laura had edited, *The Farm as Natural Habitat*. I looked through it, and Dan and his friend Jeff Klinge were in a chapter. What a coincidence!

I first visited Dan's farm, which is on a ridge close to the Mississippi River, later that year. I didn't know much about farming; I'd only been to two farms before, and, at the time, I thought of Dan as a prairie guy more than a farmer. Dan showed me his cattle, his corn, the birds, the woods.

Dan planted a prairie in 2008 close to the woods on the northeast part of the farm. The prairie is special because of the legume species–specific rhizobia (nitrogen-fixing bacteria that live inside legume roots) that Dan acquired from Peter Graham of the University of Minnesota. Dan met Peter at the 2006 North American Tallgrass Prairie Conference. Peter collected and studied soybean rhizobia from around the world for most of his career, but switched to prairie rhizobia near the end. Peter especially connected with Dan because Dan was a *farmer* interested in prairie legumes. Sadly, Peter died a few years after the conference, so the prairie with the rhizobia has even more biological significance now.

Dan changed his grazing patterns each year. He grazed the prairie during the drought of 2012. The prairie has warm-season grasses that complement the cool-season grasses in pastures. The prairie is green and nutritious when the pasture grasses are not.

Dan wanted to show that farms can feed people and be a place for nature, that working farms and conservation can go together. And ultimately, that if a farm is working with nature, the components of an ecosystem are present.

Because I live in Indiana and Dan lived in Iowa, we communicated a lot by email and phone. He would always share stories about birds he saw and plants that were flowering along the roadside. He always gave a weather report, and if the Milwaukee Brewers had played, he gave me a recap of the game. He read a lot, and followed Aldo Leopold's land ethic.

I had an eight-hour drive to visit him, so I would usually arrive at night. I would see the light in the kitchen window and feel myself relax as I drove the final stretch of gravel road. Dan would have a meal ready for me, and we would have a good conversation at the kitchen table that night and others. He would have his newsletters out and specific articles for me to read. He listened to public radio all day long. He and his brother, Phil, followed national and international news. I didn't know farmers could know so much about world affairs before I met them.

Dan had pigs for quite a few years. They were free-range on the south pasture. They would come up to the house and the big mulberry tree out the kitchen window and eat mulberries. But if they saw me looking, they would run away. They were so fun, curious, and skittish. Sometimes in the fall and winter when I visited the farm, Organic Valley would bring a truckload of outdated milk. Dan and I would go out and stab cartons of the milk, then the pigs would rip them further and drink the milk. Those pigs had a very good life. But Dan lost money on the hogs, so he eventually stopped raising them.

The year he died, he was having a good year. He had a lot of hay, and he was working with farmer Laura Krouse on delivering meat to her Community Supported Agriculture (CSA).

Dan had some rough years financially. He was a visionary and thought outside of the day-to-day world. That was a problem for him because he couldn't make himself deal with the business world. I worked with him a couple of times on spreadsheets. I had been dealing with my mom's finances, so that was becoming my world. I would ask him, "Dan, are you working on your spreadsheets?" He'd ho hum and never finish. His brother, Phil, had helped him too, but he always had late payments and late fees.

But he was always learning, like with his corn plots. For ten years he worked on developing an open-pollinated blue-and-white sweet corn. A lot of people have grown it out, including the Meskwaki Settlement in Iowa. This summer, Phil posted a wonderful poem, "My Brother's Hands," about Dan's corn and the Meskwakis' and others' interest in it.

Dan was passionate about grassland birds. These birds are in a great decline because of loss of native prairie (less than 0.1 percent of tallgrass prairie remains in Iowa) but also loss of pastureland. Birds such as the bobolink are ecological indicators of a working ecosystem, unlike a corn and bean system where most life that is not corn and beans is killed. Bobolinks migrate from South America to the northern United States to breed and return to their nesting sites from the previous year 90 percent of the time. Providing habitat for the birds is important, and some very rare prairie remnants in Missouri are being grazed by cattle in an attempt to improve habitat for the birds. I'm learning firsthand that managing the farm for birds is complex but important as an alternative to grazing prairie remnants.

The sweet song of the bobolink reminds me of Dan. He would delay haying to allow nesting pairs more time to raise their young. He would leave sacrifice patches where he wouldn't mow.

Phil, who farms nearby and now helps me with Dan's farm, is passionate about bobolinks as well. In my work as an ecologist, I would look up articles on prairies and grassland birds, and give them to Dan. Now I give articles to Phil, and we talk about them. Phil is doing his own research on and improving habitat for the birds.

Phil's and Dan's efforts are paying off. I went out to the pasture with Phil this May and noticed a bobolink. "There's one! And another!" I said. Phil said: "They are everywhere!"

After I left Dan's memorial service, I went back home, knowing that eventually the family would have to do something with the farm. Dan died without a will. I thought maybe I could buy the house and a little bit of land around the house.

The following May—May 16th—Dan's brother, Paul, who was the executor of the estate, called and said, "We're going to put the land up for auction." I couldn't speak. My initial reaction was a gut one: "No, you can't do that! What about Dan's good soils?"

I then asked if I could bid on the farm, and Paul said, "Well, there will be an auction May 23rd. There are three parcels of land, two on the main farm and another across the road. We are taking the five highest bidders for each parcel as an initial bid. Then the highest bidders will come to the bank in Monona, and there will be an auction on each of the parcels. It will be a round-robin, we'll go around, and everyone will have an option to bid higher."

I had six days to prepare for the auction, to do the financial work to determine what I could pay. Farming was not a business I understood! Dan's friend Jeff gave me some guidelines and a price that was reasonable. "The land will hold that value," he said. At the time of the sale in 2013, land prices had been going up and up and up.

Paul let me bid by phone. We did a round for one of the parcels, and I was the highest bidder. Then we did another round for the second piece, and I was the highest bidder on that one. The third round involved the land across the road to the west. Another farmer, Mike, and I kept bidding on that one. I was a little less interested in the third parcel, which was always a hay field for Dan. I don't like the herbicides, fungicides, and pesticides, and I wanted the property to protect the house. I went over the price Jeff had recommended, but then Mike bid more. So I passed, and he got the land.

But the auction wasn't over yet. Next there was an opportunity for Mike and me to raise the total bid and buy all three parcels. I was sitting there sweating. It would be a real stretch for me to buy all the land at the price I would have to bid to. I hoped Mike wouldn't bid more for the whole farm, and he didn't. The auction was over, and I was now a farmland owner.

The auction was at 10 a.m. Afterward, I took the rest of the day off because the auction was so nerve-racking. Later that day I saw a bald eagle and thought, "That's Dan flying up there."

Now I am sad I couldn't buy that third piece across the road. Mike cut the woods in the valley and plowed the hay field and later planted it to corn. "Dan, I'm so sorry," I said when I first saw it. So now I don't look to the west anymore; I look to the east when I visit the farm.

The 120 acres I purchased will be managed the way that Dan would have. He was a farmer and I am an ecologist, so we have different backgrounds, but we had a similar vision for caring for the earth. I want to include more fencerow and shrub plantings. I want to plant more prairie. I want to keep the organic certification for the farm. I want to take soil samples for a baseline of Dan's good soils and learn what happens to them over time.

I would like to continue the grazing, the habitat for grassland birds, and continue participating in the Conservation Stewardship Program (CSP). Dan worked for years to get that program passed, to help farmers get paid for conservation on working lands (rather than retiring land from farming, like the Wetlands Reserve Program, for example). I want to make sure that the CSP benefits his farm.

I will try to maintain the integrity of the grasslands and improve biodiversity and habitat, just like Dan was trying to do. That is my hope.

When I visited the farm when Dan was alive, I would take my lawn chair out and sit and watch the birds. I still do, and sit there thinking, "This is my farm now, my responsibility now."

My Brother's Hands *by Phil Specht, McGregor, Iowa*

Phil Specht

They touched seed
that embraced earth
love given birth
in circles
within circles.
Wisdom to choose
when in intercession
of sacred reach
mother to sky
sky to rock pestle, mortar
It is an old dance
corn leaves, drums
hawk, summer sun
seed to seed to seed
blessing all who touch
Let the blue sky
the blue water
blue corn
flow back to sisters
who brought forth time.

Food and Fun for Years to Come

by Leon and Marilyn Isakson, Charles City, Iowa

To Rhonda and Lon,

Leon and I purchased the 40-acre home on 130th Street in 1967 from Charlie and Amy Quade. We were living in Charles City at that time, and the Quades were looking to move from their farm to town. So we worked out a trade through a lawyer and made the move on April 1. Lloyd Krumrey farmed it that year, as he had been renting the land.

We were friends of Bob and Rosie Roeming, whose parents owned 80 acres adjoining the airport. Dorothy had contracted glaucoma, therefore Irving could no longer farm. He asked Leon if he would like to use his machinery for the first year, and just like that we were farmers! We rented that land for thirty-nine years and paid rent to three different generations. First to Dorothy and Irving, then to Rosie, and last of all to Rosie's children, Gina and Steve Roeming. In the early 1990s, the airport bought 5 acres off the 80, leaving us with 75 acres and an easement on another 5 acres that could not have corn planted on it. These 5 acres have been in either beans or hay ever since. In 2006, they became available for sale, and we used a lot of our savings and purchased them. We then invested in tiling them, and what a difference that has made! Good crops in wet and dry years!

We have now lived on our home farm for forty-eight years. We have ten Black Angus cows and a Black Angus bull. Leon raises the calves until they are ready to be butchered. He has a long list of customers who want beef that is raised without antibiotics. We raise mostly hay on this farm for feed for the cows and calves. On our other farm, we raise corn and soybeans and a small amount of hay.

Leon owned and operated Isakson Construction from 1968 to 2000. During this time, I received my B.A. degree in elementary education and taught until 2003.

During the 1970s and early 1980s, Leon raised veal calves and sheep. This was a lot of extra work while he was working away from the home during the day, so we sold the sheep and stopped raising the veal calves.

In 1979, we built a pond in our pasture and planted a 2-acre forest preserve in the northeast corner of the farm. We planted hickory and oak trees, and by now they are very tall, and the turkeys and deer enjoy the acorns they produce.

Leon built the basement of our new house in 1971 and the upstairs in 1977. In 2000, just before he retired, we put an addition on the house, including a garage and a three-season room and new living room.

Leon was born in Estherville, Iowa, and I was born in Clarion, Iowa. He spent a lot of time with his grandparents on their farm in Emmet County and grew to love the farm and all the work that goes with it. As soon as we bought our house in Charles City, he began to look for an acreage for us. At that time, he was working for Western Union as an office manager.

All the buildings on our farm have had steel put on them, and additions were put on some of them. We put up the Harvestore [for feed storage] in 1970, which helped make the workload lighter. We purchased all used Allis-Chalmers (AC) machinery to get started. We have four AC tractors, the newest one a 1967 190XT, which he uses mostly for field work. He is a man with problem-solving skills and is not afraid to try new things. Mostly he learns by doing.

Visual memories of our farm include the tidiness of our place. Most of the time, machinery is kept in the sheds. Leon does all our mowing, trimming, and keeping the flower beds looking nice. He has a special talent for parking machinery in the sheds, leaving little space between them. Our two gardens are a partner project: Leon does the tilling, and I do the weeding and canning and freezing of vegetables for our winter food. I bake most all our bread and love to bake anything else as well. You can often smell something in the oven when you come to our place. I like to buy my spices, oatmeal, and other baking supplies at the Mennonite store a few miles from us. I also love the smell of newly mown hay and the soil being turned over in the fall or spring. There is one smell in our neighborhood we are not fond of, and that is a 4,000-head hog confinement built in 2001.

The sound of the tractors and other machinery working in the fields is a good one. Also the birdsongs are fun to listen to when I am on my walks. When the cows have their babies, they make a special sound, kind of a lowing sound.

Some major events in our lives on this farm have been the time my cousins all brought their campers and we had a reunion here. There were about twenty of us, and we had such a good time. We often have friends over during the summer and sit down at our pond around a campfire. It is a whole different world down there! The blue heron sometimes flies up in the willow tree near us, and we can see the deer and the other wild animals sometimes too. The fish jump sometimes, and sometimes the pond is real quiet.

Leon is a believer in crop rotation and building the soil. It is important to us that our farm continues to be managed in this way. His cattle are always well fed and bedded. We say he has contented cows. We do spray for weed control and plant Roundup Ready beans and corn. Our machinery is all kept in good working order. If Leon can't fix it, he knows someone who can.

Thirty years from now, we want people to remember the tidiness of our farm, that it's been in our family for a lot of years, and all the fun we've had working and playing together on it. Summers were filled with happy grandchildren learning about the garden and having fun in the wide-open spaces. We treasure those days.

Our farm goal is to provide land for our farming heirs while providing compensation to the ones who do not choose to farm. We want our family to continue to enjoy times together. This goal is important to us because we have worked hard to make this place one that will provide food and fun for years to come.

We leave you with this message: we love all of you very much and want you to enjoy life as much as we have.

We love you,

Dad and Mom

APPENDIX A **About Practical Farmers of Iowa**

Founded in 1985, Practical Farmers of Iowa uses farmer-led investigation and information sharing to help farmers practice an agriculture that benefits both the land and people.

Practical Farmers of Iowa has a vision:

Farms that are prized for their diversity of crops and livestock, their wildlife, healthy soils, innovations, beauty, and productivity;
Their connection to a rich past and a fulfilling present, where individuals and families are earning a good living;
Food that is celebrated for its connections to local farmers, to seasons, to hard work and good stewardship;
Communities alive with diverse connections between farmers and friends of farmers;
Places where commerce, cooperation, creativity, and spirituality are thriving;
Places where the working landscape, the fresh air, and the clean water remind us of all that is good about Iowa.

Practical Farmers of Iowa welcomes everyone and represents a diversity of farmers and friends of farmers. Farmers in the network raise corn and soybeans, cover crops, small grains, hay, livestock large and small, horticultural crops from fruits and vegetables to cut flowers and herbs, and more. Members have conventional and organic systems, employ diverse management practices, run operations of all sizes, and come from a range of backgrounds. These farmers come together because they believe in nature as the model for agriculture and they are committed to moving their operations toward sustainability.

The organization is highly productive, offering more than 100 events each year. It focuses on farmers as leaders, sharing their expertise on stewardship, profitability, and community. The staff of Practical Farmers of Iowa is privileged to receive comments like these from its membership:

"We are learning so much by paying attention to the work PFI does."
"This is a group of intelligent people who are thought-provoking and heart-warming to be around."
"I would not be farming without Practical Farmers of Iowa."

The best testimonial for this organization? All of the stories in this book come from members of Practical Farmers of Iowa.

For more, visit: www.practicalfarmers.org.

What Matters Most for the Future of Your Farmland?

Here are common goals that farmland owners have for the future of their farmland:

- Keep family harmony
- Provide land for my farming heir(s) to farm
- Provide a farm for a family to work
- Help provide my heirs with greater financial stability through the sale of, or rental income from, the farm
- Use my farmland to benefit a charitable cause
- Give all my heirs an inheritance of equal economic value
- Keep the farmland in my family
- Use the farmland for conservation
- Other

INSTRUCTIONS:

1. Read through the goals. Change their wording, if needed, so that they all make sense to you.
2. Is there a goal missing? If so, write it down in the "Other" category.
3. Cross out the goals that are not relevant or are very low priorities for the future of your farmland.
4. Look through the remaining goals and circle your top three.
5. Examine those top three. Which is your very top goal? Put a star by it.
6. Fill out section 3 of the Farm Legacy Letter [see next appendix]. Also, ask yourself, Will your current legal and financial strategies for farm transfer help you accomplish your top farmland goal?

For more information, visit: practicalfarmers.org/member-priorities /farm-transfer.

APPENDIX C **Write Your Own Farm Legacy Letter**

On paper or on your computer, please provide the following information. Then share it with your heirs to start a conversation about the future of your farmland.

Date: _____

SECTION 1: (farm basics, the "nuts and bolts")
My farm is _____ acres located:
I have owned the farm since:
Enterprises on the farm include:
We used to have the following enterprises on the farm:
My farm has changed over the years in the following ways:

SECTION 2: (strong memories and events, the "heart and soul")
My strongest memories of the farm are:
I remember best these sights/smells/sounds/touches/tastes:
These events stand out as particularly important about the farm:

SECTION 3: (from results of goal-setting activity
    [in previous appendix], "vision for the future")
My number one goal for my farmland is:
This is my very top goal because:
The following goals are also my priorities (although not my top goal):
These are important goals for me because:

SECTION 4: (conclusion, the "parting gifts")
It is important that my farm is managed like this:
Thirty years from now, I want people to remember this about my farm:
Lastly, I want to leave you with this information:

For more information, visit: practicalfarmers.org/member-priorities
/farm-transfer.

RESOURCES

These websites are good places to start for more information on farm transfer, as they include links to many farm transfer resources:

Practical Farmers of Iowa: Practicalfarmers.org/member-priorities/farm-transfer

The Farm Transitions Network: Farmtransitions.org

Land for Good: Landforgood.org

Land Stewardship Project:
 Landstewardshipproject.org/morefarmers/farmtransitiontools

NOTES

Chapter 1

1. Michael Duffy, *Farmland Ownership and Tenure Report* (Ames: Iowa State University, 2012).
2. USDA NASS ACH 12-27/September 2015, http://www.agcensus.usda.gov /Publications/2012/Online_Resources/Highlights/TOTAL/TOTAL_Highlights .pdf.
3. For more on Helen's work, see www.gunderfriend.com.
4. Joshua Rogers, "Dirt Cheap? Investors Are Plowing into Farmland: Here's Why," *Forbes Magazine*, September 23, 2014.
5. David Kesmodel and Jesse Newman, "Farmland Investments Take Root," *Wall Street Journal*, August 4, 2015.

Chapter 2

1. USDA Census of Agriculture, 2012.
2. American Farm Bureau Federation, "Adequate Land Ranks as Top Concern of Young Farmers," *The Voice of Agriculture*, 2013, http://www.fb.org/index.php ?action=newsroom.news&year=2013&file=nr0307.html; L. L. Shute, "Building a Future with Farmers: Challenges Faced by Young American Farmers and a National Strategy to Help Them Succeed," Tivoli, NY: National Young Farmers Coalition, 2011, http://www.youngfarmers.org/.
3. John Baker, M. Duffy, and A. Laberti, *Farm Succession in Iowa* (Ames: Beginning Farmer Center, Iowa State University Extension, 2000).
4. USDA NASS ACH 12-27/September 2015, http://www.agcensus.usda.gov /Publications/2012/Online_Resources/Highlights/TOTAL/TOTAL_Highlights .pdf.
5. Ibid.
6. Ibid.
7. H. Frederick Gale, "Age-Specific Patterns of Exit and Entry in U.S. Farming, 1978–1997," *Review of Agricultural Economics* 25, no. 1 (2003).
8. R. Parsons et al., *Research Report and Recommendations from the FarmLASTS Project*, 2000, http://www.uvm.edu/farmlasts/?Page=research.html.
9. Baker et al., *Farm Succession in Iowa*.
10. Margaret J. Pitts et al., "Dialectical Tensions Underpinning Family Farm Succession Planning," *Journal of Applied Communications Research* 37, no. 1 (2009).
11. Kevin Spafford, *Legacy by Design: Succession Planning for Agribusiness Owners* (Columbia, MD: Marketplace Books, 2006).
12. Ethan Epley, M. Duffy, and J. Baker, *Iowa Farmers' Business and Transfer Plans* (Ames: Beginning Farmer Center, Iowa State University, 2009).

13. American Farmland Trust/New England Office, *Gaining Insights, Gaining Access Project* (transcripts, 2015).

14. Thérèse Aschkenase et al., "Quantitative and Qualitative Research Report" (Salt Lake City: Social Marketing Consultants for the FarmLASTS Project, 2011).

Chapter 7

1. Community Supported Agriculture involves growers and consumers providing mutual support and sharing the risks and benefits of food production. Typically, members or "shareholders" of the farm or garden pledge in advance to cover the anticipated costs of the farm operation and the farmer's salary. In return, they receive shares in the farm's bounty throughout the growing season, as well as satisfaction gained from reconnecting to the land and participating directly in food production. Members also share in the risks of farming, including poor harvests due to unfavorable weather or pests. By direct sales to community members who have provided the farmer with working capital in advance, growers receive better prices for their crops, gain some financial security, and are relieved of much of the burden of marketing. See http://afsic.nal.usda.gov/community-supported-agriculture-3.

Chapter 12

1. Neil explains: "The point here is that you don't pay all the capital gains tax at once with the sale but instead pay a slice each year with the installment payment as the income and gain are realized—this is another reason why installment contracts are a good deal: they postpone tax obligations and work like a retirement fund with annual payments."

INDEX